WORDS
FROM HEAVEN

Close-up view of the huge concrete cross on Mount Krizevak near Medjugorje erected in 1933 in honor of the 1900th anniversary of the death
of Our Lord. This cross dominates the entire countryside.

WORDS FROM HEAVEN

Messages of Our Lady from Medjugorje

A DOCUMENTED RECORD OF THE MESSAGES AND THEIR
MEANINGS GIVEN BY OUR LADY IN MEDJUGORJE TO THE
SIX VISIONARIES AND TWO INNER LOCUTIONISTS

by

Two Friends of Medjugorje

*"...Little Children, read everyday the messages
I gave you and transform them into life. I love
you and this is why I call you to the way of salvation with God."*
—From Our Lady's Message
of December 25, 1989

SAINT JAMES PUBLISHING
Birmingham, Alabama

The publisher realizes and accepts that the final authority regarding the Medjugorje Apparitions rests with the Holy See of Rome. We willing submit to that judgement.

--The Publisher

Publishing History
First printing February, 1990--10,000 copies
Second printing April, 1990--10,000 copies
Third printing July, 1990--10,000 copies
Fourth printing January, 1991--10,000 copies
Fifth printing June, 1991--10,000 copies

Published by Saint James Publishing

Copyright (c) 1991 Saint James Publishing

Library of Congress Catalog Card No: 89-92808

ISBN: 1-878909-02-9

DTTUMAKCTJAM February, 1990

Printed and bound in the United States of America.

For additional copies write to--

SAINT JAMES PUBLISHING
P.O. Box 380244
Birmingham, Alabama 35238-0244

ACKNOWLEDGEMENT

God alone deserves the credit for the publication of this book. It is from Him that the messages are allowed to be given through Our Lady to all of mankind. He alone deserves the praise and honor.

PUBLISHER'S PREFACE

The two authors' first estimates regarding the time it would take to publish this book was two or three months. Now, two years and thousands of hours of research later, it is realized that the original estimate was greatly underestimated. So it is with Medjugorje. It's importance is constantly underestimated. Father Jozo has said that Medjugorje is always bigger than you think. Soon after starting WORDS FROM HEAVEN, it was realized that it was not going to be an easy task. It was bigger than first thought.

The work involved translating messages from Croatian and other languages into English, cross referencing with many other translations, changing, verifying, and researching. All this took an enormous amount of time - necessary time to present to the reader the most pure, the most accurate messages of Our Lady. The authors plan to continue to revise, to recheck, and to reexamine the original Croatian when possible to always obtain the purest translation of Our Lady's messages. Why? Our Lady said:

". . . YOU NEED THE SPIRIT OF TRUTH TO BE ABLE TO CONVEY THE MESSAGES JUST THE WAY THEY ARE, NEITHER ADDING ANYTHING TO THEM, NOR TAKING ANYTHING WHATSOEVER AWAY FROM THEM, BUT JUST THE WAY I SAID THEM." (June 9, 1984)

Each message was painstakingly analyzed to make certain it was as close to the way Our Lady spoke it in Croatian. This is so important because Our Lady spoke about mysteries in Her messages. If the messages are not correct, or if they are changed, even a little, the reader may not discover what Our Lady is trying to convey. Sometimes, one Croatian word may have as many as five possible English translations. It is not enough that translators know Croatian and English. In order to obtain a pure translation, it is necessary that the translators know as much as possible about Medjugorje, Our Lady's plans, and what Our Lady means by a certain phrase. Only then can the precise word or words be translated. Sometimes this meant going directly to the source, the visionaries.

With almost one thousand separate messages in WORDS FROM HEAVEN, we know there will be some mistakes in this book. Yet it is the largest and most accurate book to date containing the messages of the Virgin Mary. It is hoped that all the effort and prayers put into this book will be a valuable tool in your conversion and help you to understand the greatness of Our Lady's messages.

--Saint James Publishing

TABLE OF CONTENTS

PART I

PART II

PART III

PART I

MEDJUGORJE
OUR LADY'S PLAN
TO SAVE THE WORLD

PART I

MEDJUGORJE
OUR LADY'S PLAN
TO SAVE THE WORLD

Since 1981 Our Lady has appeared daily in Medjugorje. Everyday She prays. Everyday She speaks. What is the message She speaks? This is what we would like to discover now. From June 1981 to April 1984 the Blessed Virgin Mary talked to the visionaries and answered their questions. Those years were the years of the birth of the message. From March 1, 1984 until the beginning of 1987, Our Lady gave a weekly message to the Parish of Medjugorje and to all people throughout the world who wanted to live Her messages. From January 25, 1987 She has been giving a monthly message on the twenty-fifth of each month. As we enter 1991, we are still receiving these monthly messages.

Why is She appearing and giving messages for such a long period of time? Our Lady's answer is:

"Dear children, you know that for your sake I have remained a long time so I might teach you how to make progress on the way of holiness." (January 1, 1987)

Our Lady has remained in Medjugorje so long to teach us holiness; that is why we call Medjugorje "the School of Holiness." She cannot teach us holiness in a few weeks or years; it takes a long time because we are slow to respond. It is difficult for us to be transformed.

After each weekly or monthly message since 1984, Our Lady says:

"Thank you for having responded to my call."

1

The word, "POZIV," in Croatian means a "call." Our Lady is thankful because we answer Her call. Her call is Her message. In other words, **"Thank you for your readiness to live my messages."** First She thanks the visionaries, then the Parish, then every person who lives the message. Her call is important. That is why She repeats Her thanks in <u>each message.</u> This is no accident. Our Lady is not just trying to be polite. It is more than that. This means: thank you for living my message, because this call, this message, is important. She appears to help us to live the message:

> **"Dear children, it is for your sake that I have stayed this long so I could help you to fulfill all the messages which I am giving you."** (October 30, 1986)

"POZIV" in Croation also means "invitation." The translation of this sentence would then be: **"Thank you for responding to my invitation."** Here again, Our Lady's invitation is Her message but it is also an <u>invitation to come.</u> The invitation to come is for the visionaries first. They come everyday to the apparition. Sometimes they have two apparitions a day. They are invited by the Blessed Mother on the hill at night and the visionaries respond to the invitation. **"Thank you for coming,"** says Our Lady, **"and thank you also for the pilgrims who come to Medjugorje, to the Church, and to the mountains."** This means it is important to come and this is why the Virgin Mary says, **"thank you,"** in each message. **"Thank you for coming to the spot of the apparitions."** Our Lady is happy to see people in Medjugorje. Usually when she sees a large crowd on Apparition Hill She usually says, **"I'm happy to see you in such large numbers."** Why? Our Lady gives the answer:

> **"Today I am grateful to you for your presence in this place, where I am giving you SPECIAL GRACES."** (March 25, 1987)

Come to Medjugorje to understand what special graces are! The Blessed Mother is grateful. **"Thank you,"** says She. See how She explains everything if we know how to look. It is very important for the Mother of God to see us come to Medjugorje. It is very important for Her to see us live Her messages. But what is this message, this invitation, this call?

CHAPTER 1

MEDJUGORJE: FIRST A CALL TO PRAYER

Prayer, as you may know, is the most frequent message of Our Lady in Medjugorje. It is rare not to have the word "prayer" in a message. Prayer is so important. But this world doesn't know that. Our Lady says:

> "You, dear children, are not able to understand how great the value of prayer is as long as you yourselves do not say: now is the time for prayer, now nothing else is important to me, now not one person is important to me but God. Dear children, consecrate yourselves to prayer with a special love so that God will be able to render graces back to you." (October 2, 1986)

> **"Dear children, pray, pray, pray." (October 25, 1989 and so many other times!)**

Medjugorje is: Pray! Pray! Pray! Prayer must be a daily offering to God:

> **"Let prayer, dear children, be your every day food." (May 30, 1985)**

Prayer is a powerful weapon:

> "Through fasting and prayer, one can stop wars, one can suspend the laws of nature." (July 21, 1982)

5

"In prayer, you shall find . . . the way out of every situation that has no exit." (March 28, 1985)

Over and over Our Lady asks us to pray. She asks us to understand the value and nature of prayer. Prayer is the first step in our spiritual life and everything else depends upon that. Prayer has to become a way of life. We have to discover prayer. We have to be persistent in our prayers:

"Be patient and constant in your prayers. And don't let Satan discourage you. He is working hard in the world. Be on your guard." (January 14, 1985)

Yes! Prayer is a fight against the powers of darkness, against Satan:

"Advance against Satan by means of prayer. . . . Put on the armor for battle and with the Rosary in your hand, defeat him!" (August 8, 1985)

The "armor for battle" is the strength of our prayers. Our Lady asked the prayer groups in Medjugorje to pray at least three hours a day. Why so many prayers?

"You wonder why all these prayers? Look around you, dear children, and you will see how greatly sin has dominated this earth. Pray, therefore, that Jesus conquers." September 13, 1984)

What are the prayers we should pray? Our Lady asks for the three parts of the Rosary everyday, prayers to the Holy Spirit, prayers of consecration to the Sacred Heart of Jesus and to Her Immaculate Heart. And, of course, the highest form of prayer, the Holy Mass. Prayer can change the very structures of our mentality. A real profound prayer life is a life of constant transformation. This is the key to everything Our Lady does in Medjugorje.

The <u>quality</u> of prayer is important. We have to see prayer like a real encounter with the Living God. We should pray with a living faith. Prayer should be a joy:

> "Today I call you to begin to pray the Rosary with a living faith. That way I will be able to help you. You, dear children, wish to obtain graces, but you are not praying. I am not able to help you because you do not want to get started. Dear children, I am calling you to pray the Rosary and that your Rosary be an obligation which you shall fulfill with joy. That way you shall understand the reason I am with you this long. I desire to teach you to pray." (June 12, 1986)

The Apparitions of Medjugorje, the meaning of Our Lady's presence: to teach us prayer. First, Medjugorje is a "school of prayer," then a "school of holiness." In this "school" Our Lady instructs us to **"pray with the heart."** (February 25, 1989 and so many other times):

> "Without love, dear children, you can do nothing." (May 29, 1986)

Love is the "motor" of everything. Without love we are not really alive. Therefore, we cannot pray without love. The heart is the symbol of love. Pray with the heart means: put love in the first place when you pray. To pray with the heart must be a decision: I decide to set aside everything, to concentrate, and to persevere in a pure prayer. I decide to abandon myself to God. This is what we call prayer with the heart. Prayer must be something alive and active to be a joy. Praying with the heart also means "praying with joy." There is no real spiritual life without joy:

> "Today I call you to approach prayer actively .... Prayer will be your joy: if you make a start, it won't be boring to you because you will be praying out of joy." (March 20, 1986)

But the thing is we have to start, to decide for ourselves to pray. Then God will lead us. Just get started. Put prayer in your life:

"Let prayer be life for you." (September 25, 1987)

This means let prayer be the activity which will bring real life in your lives, which will make you alive, really alive with the life of God Himself.

CHAPTER 2

MEDJUGORJE:
AN INVITATION TO EVERYONE

Our Lady started giving monthly messages in January 1987 and this first monthly message was a very important one. This message should be central in our understanding of Medjugorje. It expresses the reason for the apparitions which is "the salvation of mankind," and tells us that **"each one of us is chosen by God in order . . . to save mankind."** Our Lady starts the message with a word we translate **"Behold."** Apparently this word does not add anything to the actual meaning of the sentence. Seemingly the word is used there only to emphasize the great importance of the whole message. The visionaries think that when Our Lady speaks of **"each one,"** She speaks in fact to every sincere human being who hears this message and wants to live it. Father Jozo Zovko, the first Parish Priest of Medjugorje at the time of the first apparitions, who himself also receives apparitions of Our Lady, thinks that this call to **"each one of us to save mankind"** concerns particularly and primarily each pilgrim who comes to Medjugorje. Each pilgrim is thus invited by God and chosen to have a **"great role in God's design for the salvation of mankind."** We already knew at the very beginning that the desire of Our Lady through these apparitions is **"the conversion of the whole world."** **(June 26, 1981)** Now we hear that every human being is invited to participate in this plan of conversion. But first we have to change our lives. Here is this essential and crucial message in it's entirety:

> **"Dear children, behold, also today I want to call you to start living a new life as of today. Dear children, I want you to comprehend that God has chosen EACH ONE OF YOU, in**

9

order to use you in a great plan for the salvation of mankind. You are not able to comprehend how great your role is in God's design. Therefore, dear children, pray so that in prayer you may be able to comprehend what is God's plan through you. I am with you in order that you may be able to bring it about in all its fullness. Thank you for having responded to my call." (January 25, 1987)

Here Our Lady says that She is with us, that She appears to fulfill the plan to save mankind through each one of us. But we cannot comprehend the magnitude of it all nor our role in this plan without prayer. Then in April of the same year, She confirms:

"Pray in order that you may be able to comprehend all that I am giving here . . . . You know that without prayer you cannot comprehend all that God is planning through each one of you. Therefore, pray! I desire that through each one of you God's plan may be fulfilled." (April 25, 1987)

The Mother of God starts something new. She does it with each one of us. She cannot do it without our prayers:

"Therefore, dear children, pray, and in prayer you shall realize a new way of joy." (February 25, 1987)

She is appearing each day for us. She is appearing to help to fulfill Her plan, God's plan, to save mankind:

"Dear children, it is for your sake that I have stayed this long, so I could help you to fulfill all the messages which I am giving you." (October 30, 1986)

Again and again, without our prayers nothing is possible!

"Without your prayers, dear children, I cannot help you to fulfill the message which the Lord has given me to give you." (October 23, 1986)

Sinful human nature blocks our intelligence so we are not able to understand the greatness of our role in God's plan. Only through prayer can this veil be removed so that we can see the reality and the truth - we are chosen personally by Our Lady. In June 1981, She gave four sentences to the visionaries, but those sentences were also said for us now, today:

"I invite you. I need you. I chose you. You are important."

Yes, we are important because Our Lady has said:

"Without you I am not able to help the world." (August 28, 1986)

Without us, without our prayers and conversion, She cannot help mankind.

CHAPTER 3

THE TREMENDOUS IMPORTANCE
OF THESE APPARITIONS

Even the people of Medjugorje don't realize the importance of what is going on in their parish:

"No, you do not know how many graces God is giving you!" (May 9, 1985)

The graces that God gives through the Queen of Peace in Medjugorje are tremendous:

"God will give you gifts by which you will glorify Him till the end of your life on this earth." (June 2, 1984)

During Ivanka's last daily apparition, the Queen of Peace told her:

"No one in the world has had the grace which you, your brothers, and sisters have received." (May 7, 1985)

The apparitions in Medjugorje are unique. They represent something that was never before done by God - daily apparitions for more than nine and one-half years now. Our Lady also said that they were to be the last apparitions on earth. This statement caused some surprise, so the visionaries asked Our Lady questions about it many times and She confirmed:

"I have come to call the world to conversion for the last time. After that, I will not appear any more on this earth." (May 2, 1982)

However, this does not mean that there are no other apparitions going on now in the world while the apparitions in Medjugorje are happening. On the contrary, this is "a time of grace" where God is actively bringing men back to Him. But after the end of the Medjugorje apparitions, there won't be any more genuine apparitions on earth, **"only some false apparitions,"** says Our Lady.

We have many messages that tell us how Medjugorje is important to Our Lady. She wants Medjugorje to be an example for all parishes in the world, because this parish is special and has been chosen in a special way:

> **"This parish, which I have chosen, is special and different from others. And I am giving great graces to all who pray with the heart." (February 6, 1986)**

In 1987 Marija was asked this question by a French theologian: "Why do I have to come to Medjugorje as Our Lady is everywhere where we pray to Her?" Marija's answer was simple: "In Medjugorje Our Lady gives SPECIAL GRACES." Medjugorje is a special place, but the people of Medjugorje are a special people also:

> **"Dear children, you are a chosen people and God has given you great graces. You are not conscious of every message which I am giving you." (November 15, 1984)**

Here Our Lady speaks to the people of Medjugorje. They are a "chosen people." They are called to be the instrument of a great plan. An important intention of the Mother of God is to make all of us realize the importance of Her plan because we are not conscious of it or the greatness of it all.

According to Vicka, "What Our Lady does here has never been done before." Our Lady explains:

"I wish to keep on giving you messages as it has never been done in history from the beginning of the world." (April 4, 1985 - Holy Thursday)

Our Lady accomplishes this project, which is so great and unique and the first of its kind, through a parish, a people She has chosen. This is very clear after studying the messages as a whole. Here is one example:

"I love you and in a special way I have chosen this parish, one more dear to me than the other parishes, in which I have gladly remained when the Almighty sent me." (March 21, 1985)

Although men remain men, with all their sins and shortcomings, these men and women of this little village of Herzegovina were chosen in a very special way. Many temptations, many of the seductions of the world attack them, but they are still the chosen ones. Sin and Satan are powerful and even though the spiritual nature of the parish is in danger and may even die, the Blessed Mother continues to watch over Her chosen and dear children:

"I wish to tell you that I have chosen this parish and that I am guarding it in my hands like a little flower that does not want to die." (August 1, 1985)

At least a small number will be saved to be the witnesses of God's Peace in the world. After reading the following messages, it is obvious that Our Lady gave a special "privilege" to the parish of Medjugorje.

"I have chosen this parish in a special way and I wish to guide it. I am guarding it in love and I want everyone to be mine." (March 1, 1984)

"... Dear children, I am giving the messages first of all to the
residents of the parish, and then to all the others. . . ."
(February 6, 1986)

And this message given to Jelena (July 30, 1987):

"Dear children, to be chosen by God is really something great,
but it is also a responsibility for you to pray more, for you,
the chosen ones, to encourage others, so you can be a light for
people in darkness. . . . Dear children, this is the reason for
my presence among you for such a long time: to lead you on
the path of Jesus. I want to save you and, THROUGH YOU,
TO SAVE THE WHOLE WORLD."

This message was addressed to the parish in general and in particular
to the members of Jelena's prayer group. Our Lady wants to save
the whole world through Medjugorje.

CHAPTER 4

THE WORLD IS IN DARKNESS

In this same message to Jelena which we just quoted, the Mother of God adds:

> "Children, darkness reigns over the whole world. People are attracted by many things and they forget about the more important . . . . Many people now live without faith; some don't even want to hear about Jesus, but they still want peace and satisfaction! Children, here is the reason why I need your prayer: prayer is the only way to save the human race." (July 30, 1987)

This message sums up the spirit of Medjugorje. The entire basic message is here.

Our Lady also talks about **"this unfaithful world walking into darkness."** (June 5, 1986) Satan has a strong grip over modern society. Our Lady told Mirjana on April 4, 1982:

> **"This is the time of the devil."**

The situation of the world is bad:

> **"My Son struggles for each of you, but Satan fights Him also."** (1981)

> **"Satan exists! He seeks only to destroy."** (February 14, 1982)

> **"Satan is working hard in the world."** (January 14, 1985)

> **"Satan wants to impose hardships to the Catholic Church."** (June 25, 1985)

"Dear children, do not allow Satan to get control of your hearts so you would be an image of Satan and not of me." (January 30, 1986)

"Satan is strong and is waiting to test each one of you." (September 25, 1987)

Although there is a long list of messages about Satan, Our Lady does not want to paint a picture of hopelessness in describing the power of the devil in our world. On the contrary, She wants to give us weapons against the Powers of Darkness. But we have to see the situation with lucidity: Satan is powerful, he wants to seduce us. He is active in the world. According to Our Lady, Satan is also very present in the Parish of Medjugorje. Satan knows he can have a strong and decisive victory if he can stop or injure severely the plans of the Mother of God in Medjugorje itself. Here is one message among many which Our Lady gave to Mirjana on January 28, 1987. In this message The Blessed Mother speaks to the Parish of Medjugorje:

"Whenever I come to you my Son comes with me, but so does Satan. You permitted, without noticing, his influences on you and he drives you on."

Actually Satan by his work did destroy part of the plan of Our Lady in Medjugorje:

"Satan has taken away one part of the plan and he wants to possess it." (August 1, 1985)

But a month later, after a strong effort in prayer by the parish, Our Lady said:

"Today I thank you for all the prayers. Keep on praying all the more so that Satan will be far away from this place. Dear children, Satan's plan has failed. Pray for the fulfillment of what God plans in this parish." (September 5, 1985)

CHAPTER 5

THE PLAN OF OUR LADY AGAINST SATAN

Prayer has defeated Satan's plan. Prayer is the first weapon against Satan. Our Lady wants us to use five weapons (described below) to overcome the power of Satan in our lives and in the world. This is her "Peace Plan":

"You are ready to commit sin, and to put yourselves in the hands of Satan without reflecting." (May 25, 1987)

This is the picture of modern society.

"The peace of the world is in danger." (1981)

This was the picture of modern world. Now (we write in 1989) this situation about world peace seems to be improving. Thanks to prayers. Because Our Lady said:

"Dear children, without prayer there is no peace. Therefore, I say to you, dear children, pray at the foot of the crucifix for peace." (September 6, 1984)

We can change the world through prayer. It is very important for us to realize that.

THE FIRST WEAPON AGAINST SATAN: PRAYER

We talk about that all the time. This is the center of Our Lady's plan: prayer! Again, this is the most frequent message in Medjugorje. Let us quote just a few more simple messages about prayer:

"Today also I am calling you to prayer. You know, dear
children, that God grants special graces in prayer. . . . I call
you, dear children, to prayer with the heart." (April 25, 1987)

To pray with the heart is to pray with abandonment, love, and trust
and with concentration also. Prayer heals. Prayer heals human souls.
Prayer heals history [history of sin]. Without prayer, we cannot have
an experience of God:

"Without unceasing prayer you cannot experience the beauty
and greatness of the grace which God is offering you."
(February 25, 1989)

What are the prayers Our Lady recommends? The three parts of the
Rosary everyday, the Adoration of the Holy Sacrament, prayers to the
Holy Spirit (especially before Mass), prayers in front of the crucifix,
prayers of consecration to the Sacred Heart of Jesus and to the
Immaculate Heart of Mary. Everybody should pray. Our Lady says:

"May prayer reign in the whole world." (August 25, 1989)

In this way, through prayer, we will defeat Satan's power, obtain
peace and salvation for our souls:

You know that I love you and am coming here out of love, so
I could show you the path of peace and salvation for your
souls. I want you to listen to me and not permit Satan to
seduce you. Dear children, Satan is strong enough!
Therefore, I ask you to dedicate your prayers so that those
who are under his influence may be saved. Give witness by
your life, sacrifice your lives for the salvation of the world . .
. . Therefore, little children, do not be afraid. If you pray,
Satan cannot injure you, not even a little, because you are
God's children and He is watching over you. Pray, and let the
rosary always be in your hands as a sign to Satan that you
belong to me." (February 25, 1988)

The power of Satan is destroyed by prayer and he cannot harm us if we pray. That is why no Christian should be afraid of the future, unless he does not pray. And if he does not pray, is he a Christian? If we do not pray, we are naturally blind to many things; we cannot tell right from wrong. We lose our center; we lose our balance.

THE SECOND WEAPON AGAINST SATAN: FASTING

A message about fasting appeared on the third day of the apparitions when the Virgin said to Marija that to achieve peace, ". . . **it is necessary to believe, to pray, to fast and to go to confession."** (June 26, 1981)

In the Old Testament and in the New Testament, we see many examples of fasting. Jesus fasted. According to Tradition, fasting is encouraged especially in times of great temptation or severe trials. Certain devils, "can be cast out in no other way except by prayer and fasting," said Jesus. (Mark 9:29)

Fasting is an instrument to overcome the power of darkness present in the world now and it has a purification value. Our time is a time of darkness, that is why we should use fasting often. Our Lady recommends it twice a week:

"Fast strictly on Wednesdays and Fridays." (August 14, 1984)

She requested us to accept this difficult message ". . . **with a firm will."** She asks us to "Persevere in . . . fasting." (June 25, 1982)

"The best fast is on bread and water. Through fasting and prayer one can stop wars, one can suspend the laws of nature. Works of charity cannot replace fasting . . . . Everyone, except the sick, has to fast." (July 21, 1982)

Again, fasting is a strong weapon against the devil:

"The devil tries to impose his power on you, but you must
remain strong and persevere in your faith. You have to pray
and fast. I will always be close to you." (November, 1981)

"The devil is trying to conquer you. Do not permit him. Keep
faith, fast, and pray. I will be with you at every step."
(November 16, 1981)

Fasting is recommended in times of special trouble or for difficult
situations:

"Pray for Father Jozo [who was in jail] and fast tomorrow on
bread and water." (October 19, 1981)

We have to "fast for the sick" to obtain their healing. (August 18,
1982)

"For the cure of the sick, it is important to say the following
prayers: the Creed, and seven times each, The Lord's Prayer,
the Hail Mary, and the Glory Be, and to fast on bread and
water." (July 25, 1982)

Our Lady also asked some special fasting for the Bishop of Mostar
who does not believe in the apparitions:

"Fast two days a week for the intentions of the Bishop, who
bears a heavy responsibility. If there is a need to, I will ask
for a third day." (July, 1983)

Each visionary has or will receive ten secrets. Some of those secrets
concern chastisement or warnings to mankind because of its sins. In
regard to one of the secrets that concerned a catastrophe, Our Lady
told Mirjana:

"I have prayed; the punishment has been softened. Repeated
prayers and fasting reduce punishments from God."
(November 6, 1982)

We have to realize the power of fasting. Fasting means to make a sacrifice for God, to offer not only our prayers, but also to make our whole being, our body itself, participate in sacrifice. And we do that with love, for a special intention, and to purify ourselves and the world. This great task of purification needs sacrifices. We do not offer it because we must; we offer it because we love God and want to be courageous soldiers that also offer our bodies in the battle against evil.

THE THIRD WEAPON AGAINST SATAN: DAILY READING OF THE BIBLE

Usually Our Lady comes to the visionaries "happy and joyful," as Ivan puts it after each apparition. But on some occasions Our Lady has appeared being very sad. On other very rare occasions She has cried. One time She cried when She was talking about the Bible. Father Jozo says that as a priest he saw many mothers mourning their sons at funerals, but he never saw a mother so sad as the Mother of God when She talked about the Bible. Those tears are terrible tears. While crying, Our Lady said:

"You have forgotten the Bible."

The Bible is a book different from any other book on earth. Vatican II says that all the canonical books of the Bible were, ". . . written under the inspiration of the Holy Spirit, they have God as their author." (Dogmatic Constitution on Divine Revelation, Chapter 3.) This means that no other book can be compared to this book. That is why Our Lady asks us to separate THE BOOK from the other human books on the shelves. There is no writing even from a saint or inspired that can be compared to the Bible. That is why we are asked to place the Bible in a visible separate place in our homes:

"Dear children, today I call you to read the Bible everyday in your homes and let it be in a visible place so as always to encourage you to read it and to pray." (October 18, 1984)

It is very rare to hear Our Lady say, **"you must."** She "desires,"
"calls," etc., but on one occasion She used a very strong Croatian verb
that means "must":

> **"Every family must pray family prayers and read the Bible."**
> **(February 14, 1985)**

THE FOURTH WEAPON AGAINST SATAN: CONFESSION

Our Lady asks for monthly confession. From the very first days of
the apparitions, Our Lady spoke about confession:

> **"Make your peace with God and among yourselves. For that,**
> **it is necessary to believe, to pray, to fast, and to go to**
> **confession." (June 26, 1981)**

> **"Pray, pray! It is necessary to believe firmly, to go to**
> **confession regularly, and, likewise, to receive Holy**
> **Communion. It is the only salvation." (February 10, 1982)**

The Mother of God stressed the force of repentance:

> **"Whoever has done very much evil during his life can go**
> **straight to Heaven if he confesses, is sorry for what he has**
> **done, and receives Communion at the end of his life." (July**
> **24, 1982)**

The Western Church has disregarded confession and its importance
and concerning this Our Lady said:

> **"Monthly confession will be a remedy for the Church in the**
> **West. One must convey this message to the West." (August**
> **6, 1982)**

A pilgrim who comes to Medjugorje is always impressed by the
number of people waiting for confession and the number of priests

hearing confessions. Many priests have had extraordinary experiences during confessions in Medjugorje. Our Lady said the following about confessions during a certain feast day:

"The priests who will hear confessions will have great joy on that day! (August, 1984)

But confession should not be a habit that would actually "make sinning easy." Vicka says to every group of pilgrims, "Confession is something that has to make a new human being out of you. Our Lady does not want you to think that confession will free you from sin and allow you to continue the same life after that. No, confession is a call to transformation. You must become a new person!" Our Lady explained the same idea to Jelena:

"Do not go to confession through habit, to remain the same after it. No, it is not good. Confession should give an impulse to your faith. It should stimulate you and bring you closer to Jesus. If confession does not mean anything for you, really, you will be converted with great difficulty." (November 7, 1983)

FIFTH WEAPON AGAINST SATAN: THE EUCHARIST

Our Lady also cried when She spoke about the Eucharist and the Mass. In 1985 She said:

"You do not celebrate the Eucharist as you should. If you would know what grace and what gifts you receive, you would prepare yourselves for it each day for an hour at least."

The evening Mass in Medjugorje is the most important moment of the day because Our Lady is present and She gives us Her Son in a special way. The Mass is more important than the daily apparition. Marija said that if she had to choose between the Eucharist and the apparition, she would choose the Eucharist. Our Lady said:

"The evening Mass must be kept permanently." (October 6, 1981)

She also asked that the prayer to the Holy Spirit always be said before Mass. Our Lady wants us to see the Holy Mass as "the highest form of prayer" and "the center of our lives," (according to Marija's words). Vicka also says that the Blessed Mother sees the Mass as "the most important and the most holy moment in our lives. We have to be prepared and pure to receive Jesus with a great respect. The Mass should be the center of our lives." Our Lady is crying because people do not have enough respect toward the Eucharist. The Mother of God is sad and cries especially because we do not realize the extreme beauty of the mystery of Mass. But She rejoices because:

"There are many of you who have sensed the beauty of the Holy Mass . . . . Jesus gives you His graces in the Mass." (April 3, 1986)

Our Lady has come to give us the Living and Resurrected Jesus:

"Let the Holy Mass be your life." (April 25, 1988)

This means that the sacrifice and resurrection of Christ must become our life, together with the hope of His second coming. During Mass, we receive the Living Christ and in Him we receive the whole mystery of our salvation that must transform us, transfigure us. Mass is the perfect expression of the mystery of Christ in which we can fully participate in His life:

"Mass is the greatest prayer of God. You will never be able to understand its greatness. That is why you must be perfect and humble at Mass, and you should prepare yourselves for it." (1983)

Our Lady wants us to be full of joy and hope during Mass and to make an effort so that this moment will **"be an experience of God."**

(May 16, 1985.) Surrender to Jesus and to the Holy Spirit is a very important part of the messages, because, as we will see, it is the only way to holiness. To be open to the Holy Spirit in the Sacraments is the way we are going to be sanctified. In this way, Our Lady will obtain for us the grace so that we can become Her witnesses in the world to fulfill the plan of God and Her plan:

"Open your hearts to the Holy Spirit. Especially during these days the Holy Spirit is working through you. Open your hearts and surrender your life to Jesus so that He works through your hearts." (May 23, 1985)

CHAPTER 6

"I AM THE QUEEN OF PEACE"

The first call and invitation of Our Lady is peace. She said on the third day of Her apparitions:

"Peace, Peace, Peace! Be reconciled! Only Peace. Make your peace with God and among yourselves. For that, it is necessary to believe, to pray, to fast, and to go to confession."

Marija received this message on June 26, 1981, after she had the apparition with the other visionaries on top of Apparition Hill. On returning to the village, about half way from the bottom of the hill, Marija saw the Virgin again. Our Lady was very sad and held a crucifix with rainbow colors. Later the Mother of God said that Her name for these Apparitions of Medjugorje was "The Queen of Peace." Then on Monday, August 24, 1981, many people in Medjugorje, including Father Jozo Zovko, saw a large inscription in the sky on top of Mount Krizevac. The word "MIR" appeared in large burning letters. "MIR" is Croatian for "peace." This is the central message of Medjugorje.

What is the meaning of the word "peace" in Christian tradition? In Hebrew, "shalom" indicates an idea of wholeness and unity. Jerusalem, for instance, means the "City of Peace," or more accurately, the "Seeing of Peace." This city is symbolically the place of unity between God and man. In Psalm 122, we have a song of peace for the "City of Peace." And in verse 3, we find the idea of wholeness and harmony: "Jerusalem built as a city with compact unity." Jerusalem is the place of peace not only because it is one, and united as a city, but also because this city is called to have complete unity with God, to be in harmony with God. From all this we can discover the real meaning of peace. Peace is harmony between God and man.

"Shalom" also includes the idea of happiness, joy, and prosperity. But real happiness, joy, and prosperity can come only through this peace, which comes from God and is a direct gift from the Holy Spirit:

> **"When the Holy Spirit comes, peace will be established."** (October, 1984)

Our Lady says:

> **"Live peace in your heart and in your surroundings, so that all recognize peace, which does not come from you, but from God."** (Christmas-Day message, 1988)

Vicka says that Our Lady loves the feast of Christmas very much. She always appears on Christmas in golden vestments with Baby Jesus in Her arms, with immense joy. She gave one of Her main messages about peace on Christmas day:

> **"Celebrate the birth of Jesus with my peace, the peace with which I came to you as your Mother, Queen of Peace."** (December, 1988)

Christmas time is a period of harmony between God and man because God becomes man! Christmas, Our Lady says, **". . . is a great day. Rejoice with me!"** (December 25, 1988) Here we find the joy aspect of peace, peace brought to every creature by the Incarnation which brings harmony in the world. At Christmas we feel and live this special spirit of harmony and beauty where the whole creation is as if touched by the love of God. The angels sang, "Glory to God in the highest and on earth PEACE to those on whom His favor rests." (Luke 2:14) From this quote, we receive an even more clear bit of information about the nature of peace. Peace is a relationship between God and man. Peace is harmony between God in the highest who incarnates Himself to become man, and human beings who receive peace and blessing from above. Christmas has a lot to do with unity and harmony between heaven and earth. Peace is a blessing from God. Our Lady wants us to extend Her own blessing to all to help the harmony to come to reality. On Christmas day, 1988, She said:

> **"I am giving you my Special Blessing. Carry it to every creature so that each one may have peace."** (December 25, 1988)

Before we start to speak about the path of holiness, we have to realize that a holy person or a saint is one who has achieved peace in his heart, which means one has achieved a high degree of harmony between himself and God. Peace - harmony - is a gift from God; only God can give it:

> **". . . peace, which does not come from you, but from God."** (December 25, 1988)

Christmas is the coming of the Prince of Peace as foretold in Isaiah 9:5: "For a child is born to us, a son is given to us; upon his shoulder dominion rests. They name Him . . . Prince of Peace." And the Queen of Peace says:

> **"I call you always to bring harmony and peace."** (July 31, 1986)

If we know a little bit about what the "Christmas spirit" is, we can begin to understand what the word "PEACE" means.

CHAPTER 7

THE ONLY SOLUTION
TO HEAL THE WORLD: HOLINESS

Our Lady says:

> "Without you I am not able to help the world." (August 28, 1986)

> "I desire to lead you on the way to holiness." (October 9, 1986)

Her plan to save mankind is impossible without holiness. God always worked and saved through holiness. A period of history without saints is a period of history without God's glorious presence and God's work:

> "God has chosen each one of you in order to use you in a great plan for the salvation of mankind." (January 25, 1987)

Our Lady's presence here is to fulfill this plan for the salvation of mankind:

> "I am with you in order that you may be able to bring it about [the plan] in all its fullness." (January 25, 1987)

Our Lady's presence here is also to teach us holiness, because, once again, without holiness there is no salvation of mankind:

> "Dear children, you know that for your sake I have remained a long time so I might teach you how to make progress on the way to holiness." (January 1, 1987)

In the same month, January 1987, through those two messages (on
the 1st and the 25th) Our Lady gave us two clues to explain the
reason for those very long Apparitions of Medjugorje: She came to
save mankind and She came to call us to holiness. There is only one
way to save mankind from the powers of darkness, from Satan. We
have to make a strong decision for God and against Satan and we
have to walk with Our Lady toward holiness. Our Lady's plan in
Medjugorje is to save mankind through holiness. The goal of Our
Lady's coming is just that: to lead us to holiness, to lead us to a
better life with God on earth, and to lead us to Heaven. The
message of May 25, 1987, sums up Her whole plan:

**"I call on each one of you to consciously decide for God and
against Satan. I am your Mother and, therefore, I want to
lead you all to complete holiness. I want each one of you to
be happy here on earth and to be with me in Heaven. That is,
dear children, the purpose of my coming here and it's my
desire."**

Actually, holiness is to live on earth as if already in Heaven. In 1986
Our Lady said to Jelena:

**"If you would abandon yourselves to me, you will not even feel
the passage from this life to the next life. You will begin to
live the life of Heaven from this earth."**

What does it mean to "walk on the path of holiness?" Holiness is a
gift from God. It is not something we can achieve by ourselves, by
our own human strength. If we accept the invitation to live the
messages of Our Lady, holiness will grow by itself inside of us;
holiness will sprout out in our hearts and this will be a gift from God.
The only thing God asks to be able to give us this gift, is our
faithfulness in living the messages and our decision to live for God
and against Satan. The gift of holiness is granted to those who make
a decision for God and who live the messages. Our Lady puts in our
hands five weapons: Prayer, Fasting, the Bible, Confession, and the
Eucharist. If we live those messages, holiness will grow in us:

**"Dear children, if you live the messages, you are living the
seeds of holiness." (October 10, 1985)**

This means holiness will grow by itself in us.

Holiness is a danger, the "greatest" danger to Satan's power. By his
witnessing and his life itself, a saint directly attacks the core of
Satan's power in the world. The fight against darkness is a battle:

**"Advance against Satan by means of prayer . . . . Put on the
armor for battle and with the rosary in your hand defeat him
(August 8, 1985)**

**"By prayer you can completely disarm him [Satan]." (January
24, 1985)**

Holiness comes from the Holy Spirit. Our Lady insists on the prayer
to the Holy Spirit, especially before Mass. The prayer to the Holy
Spirit is also said in Ivan's prayer group each time Ivan has his
apparition. Just before the apparition, the "Veni Creator Spiritus"
(Come O Spirit of Creation) is said in Croatian. We need the Holy
Spirit to become new human beings:

**"Ask the Holy Spirit to renew your souls, to renew the entire
world." (March 5, 1984)**

Through the Holy Spirit we can become a new human being and live
on the earth as if already in Heaven. The joy of the Resurrected
Christ has to dwell in our hearts:

**"Raise your hands, yearn for Jesus because in His
Resurrection He wants to fill you with graces. Be enthusiastic
about the Resurrection. All of us in Heaven are happy, but we
seek the joy of your hearts." (April 21, 1984)**

But to be enthusiastic about the Resurrection, we have to be
immersed in the reality of the Cross. A real joy of the Resurrection

may be born in our hearts only if a real love and knowledge of the fruitfulness of the cross is constantly present in us. If we spiritually participate in the sacrifice of Christ, we will be given the grace to see His victory already here on earth. Jesus must rise again in our hearts, and in our families:

"May Jesus truly rise in your families." (April 21, 1984)

We have to participate in Christ's Passion and in His Resurrection by the power of the Holy Spirit to become holy. In Holy Communion we receive Jesus Crucified and Resurrected. By the Holy Spirit we are transformed to become an image of Christ. That is why Holy Communion is life for us:

"Let the Holy Mass be your life." (April 25, 1988)

Jesus said: "I am the Resurrection and the life." (John 11:25) Through the grace of the Sacraments we receive the Holy Spirit to have light and to resemble Christ:

"I wish that you all be the reflection of Jesus, which will enlighten this unfaithful world walking in darkness." (June 5, 1986)

The highest call of Our Lady is for us to be the reflection of Jesus. By his own strength and work, nobody can be the reflection of Jesus. It can only happen if it is granted by God, through the Holy Spirit. The Holy Spirit is love and light:

"The most important thing in the spiritual life is to ask for the gift of the Holy Spirit. When the Holy Spirit comes, the peace will be established. When that occurs, everything changes around you." (October, 1984)

"Pray to the Holy Spirit for enlightenment." (November 8, 1984)

The Death and Resurrection of Jesus opened a new era to mankind in which we could receive in a special way the grace to be a light to others. On Good Friday (April 20, 1984), Our Lady said to Jelena:

> "You should be filled with joy! Today, Jesus died for your salvation. He descends to Hell and opens the gates of Paradise. Let joy reign in your hearts!"

By this joy and through this light that we receive as a gift at Baptism and with the Sacraments, we can be the witnesses of the light of Christ:

> "In your life you have all experienced light and darkness. God grants to every person recognition of good and evil. I am calling you to the light which you should carry to all the people who are in darkness. People who are in darkness daily come into your homes. Dear children, give them the light!" (March 14, 1985)

This light can only come from the Holy Spirit. Our Lady says:

> "When you have the Holy Spirit, you have everything." (October 21, 1983)

The Holy Spirit makes us holy. The Holy Spirit can make us light to others. It is especially in the Sacraments of the Church and during the Holy Mass that we can receive the Holy Spirit:

> "I wish your Mass to be an experience of God. I wish especially to say to the young people: be open to the Holy Spirit because God wishes to draw you to Himself." (May 16, 1985)

CHAPTER 8

WHAT IS HOLINESS?

Again, holiness is a gift which comes only from God, through the Holy Spirit. We cannot achieve holiness by our own strength. Holiness is growth with God. Our Lady gave a definition of holiness:

"Today I am calling you to holiness. Without holiness you cannot live. Therefore, with love overcome every sin and with love overcome all the difficulties which are coming to you. Dear children, please, live love within yourselves."
(July 10, 1986)

TO BE HOLY IS TO OVERCOME SIN BY LOVE. This is the definition of holiness. A saint does not overcome sin and difficulties through human means like the world would. A saint overcomes sin through love. The instrument we have to use always is love:

"Act with love. Let your only instrument always be love. By love turn everything into good which Satan desires to destroy and possess. Only that way shall you be completely mine and I shall be able to help you." (July 31, 1986)

Our Lady wishes us to be totally Hers. "TOTUS TUUS" (Totally Yours) is the motto that Pope John Paul II chose. The call of Mary is to abandon ourselves completely to Her and to God. This is one of the most frequent messages in Medjugorje - abandon yourselves to God. Holiness is total abandonment to the will of God! To renounce our own will and instead put the will of God in our lives is essential to holiness. Another thing is essential to holiness: to accept sacrifice. The spirit of sacrifice is an ingredient that God uses for purification and we badly need purification. Sacrifice, especially fasting, prepare our hearts to receive the gift of holiness:

"Prepare your hearts for these days when the Lord particularly desires to purify you from all the sins of your past . . . . Prepare your hearts in penance and fasting." (December 4, 1986)

If we choose holiness we should also be ready for change! We should be willing to change our lives:

"I am calling you to pray with your whole heart and day by day to change your life . . . . I am calling that by your prayers and sacrifices you begin to live in holiness . . . , daily change your life in order to become holy." (November 13, 1986)

Medjugorje then is this "School of Holiness," where holiness is available and given to each pilgrim - if he wants! The only thing we have to do is to make a decision for holiness and abandon ourselves completely to God:

"I ask you to abandon yourself completely to God." (March 25, 1989 and many, many other messages)

"Put your life in God's hands." (January 25, 1988)

The "School of Holiness" is a school of love. This is very important. Our Lady does not think we can convert the world through anything else but love. Holiness is love in action. She does not think we can change the world through science or knowledge or intelligence or human strength. We can change hearts and change the world only through love in action and through love incarnate in human beings:

"Without love, dear children, you can do nothing." (May 29, 1986)

"Without love you will achieve nothing." (December 13, 1984)

We will achieve neither holiness nor conversion without love because love is the motor of the whole process of inner transformation. The key to holiness is love:

"Make a decision for love." (November 20, 1986)

"Love makes great things." (April 12, 1987)

Holiness is the growth of love in our hearts:

"I desire to call you to grow in love. A flower is not able to grow normally without water. So also you, dear children, are not able to grow without God's blessing." (April 10, 1986)

A lot of people think that we should explain and convince the world to change its ways, that we should use intelligence, knowledge, politics, and science to make things go better. Our Lady says that we can accomplish much greater things if we use love as a tool. But the problem is that we have forgotten real love:

"No, you don't know how to love." (November 29, 1984)

This is why the Mother of God has come on the earth for eight and one-half years now (December 1989), to teach us love. And if She teaches us love, She teaches us holiness at the same time.

The sin of the world in which we live is sometimes terrible. Our mission in this world is **"to overcome every sin with love."** (July 10, 1986) A saint is the one who **"Lives love within himself."** (July 10, 1986)

First of all, we should not fear becoming a saint. As Mother Teresa of Calcutta said: "To be a saint is the duty of each Christian." To be a saint is something that comes from God, not from us. We should be faithful in living the messages and then holiness will grow in us by itself as a gift coming from Heaven. This is what Our Lady meant when She said:

"If you live the messages, you are living the seeds of holiness." (October 10, 1985)

First, live the messages; this is the first step toward holiness. Live the five main messages of Medjugorje, the five practical things you have to do in your life: Prayer, Fasting, Reading the Bible, Confession and Holy Mass. If you live these messages, you will put the seeds of holiness in your hearts. But only love can make them sprout and give fruit because:

"Without love we will achieve nothing."
(December 13, 1984)

"Love makes great things." (April 12, 1987)

What is the most important thing in life? Jesus was asked this question in the form of, "What is the most important commandment of all?" Commandments of the Law were for the Jews the most important things in life. As you know, Jesus answered, "Thou shalt love the Lord thy God with thy whole heart, and with thy whole soul, and with thy whole mind! This is the greatest and first commandment. And the second is like it. Thou shalt love thy neighbor as thyself! On these two commandments depend the whole Law and the Prophets." (Matthew 22:34-40) Our Lady, who is just repeating the Gospel for our time, says, of course, the same thing:

"Today my call to you is that in your life you live love toward God and neighbor. Without love, dear children, you can do nothing." (May 29, 1986)

Medjugorje is a constant message of love. Here are some examples which convey the message of love:

"Start loving from today with an ardent love, the love with which I love you." (May 29, 1986)

"By love you will be able to do even that which you think is impossible." (November 7, 1985)

"Today I call you to live the words, 'I love God,' during the week. Dear children, through love you will achieve everything and even what you think is impossible." (February 28, 1985)

We will achieve holiness even if we think it's impossible!

"I am calling you to love your neighbor." (November 7, 1985)

Our Lady also speaks of Her love toward us:

"I love you in a special way." (March 21, 1985)

"Today again I want to show you how much I love you, but I am sorry that I am not able to help each one to understand my love." (October 16, 1986)

We can neither imagine nor realize fully how great Our Lady's love is. Only in deep prayer and with Her blessing can we feel Her presence which is the presence of love. Many Medjugorje pilgrims have received this gift of approaching, at least a little, the immense mystery of Our Lady's great love. But She wants our love in return. Our Lady's path leads toward love; She speaks of the "way of love" (June 25, 1988); and She wants us to grow in love, which means to grow in holiness day by day:

". . . so that God's love may be able to grow in you day by day." (June 25, 1988)

We are called to perfect love:

"Pray, because in prayer each one of you will be able to achieve complete love." (October 25, 1987)

Our love must be like Our Lady's love. We have to make a decision to love. We must be strong and decisive for love:

"God does not want you lukewarm or undecided, but that you totally surrender to Him. You know that I love you and that

I am burning out of love for you. Therefore, dear children, you also make a decision for love so you will burn out of love and daily experience God's love. Dear children, decide for love so that LOVE PREVAILS IN ALL OF YOU. But not human love, rather God's love." (November 20, 1986)

CHAPTER 9

THE FRUITS OF LOVE

We could say the "fruits of conversion," or even the "fruits of holiness." The first fruits of our own conversion are joy and happiness that come from God:

> **"I am calling you to the great joy and peace which only God can give."** (March 25, 1989)

God has been giving us many gifts in Medjugorje; this should fill us with joy:

> **"Rejoice in everything you have received."** (April 25, 1989)

Through prayer, in our conversion, and with the love of God in our hearts, the world, the living reality around us, and all creation reveal their secrets. A life with God is a life of discovery in which we discover God Himself in His creation:

> **"You will discover God in everything, even in the smallest flower. You will discover a great joy. You will discover God!"** (April 25, 1989)

The abundance of what God gives us if we abandon ourselves to Him is amazing. The joy of the love of God is something that can save the world, and Our Lady wants us to be the witnesses of that:

> **"Be strong in God. I desire that through you the whole world may get to know the God of joy."** (May 25, 1988)

The witnessing of Our Lady's messages is a mission by which we are called to save the world. We have to be witnesses of joy. Again and again, we know we are called to be witnesses to save the world:

"God has chosen each one of you in order to use you in a great plan for the salvation of mankind." (January 25, 1987)

The whole meaning of the apparitions is contained here. How can we **"bring harmony and peace"** (July 31, 1986) to the world? We must unite our lives with God's life. We do that through Sacraments, especially Holy Communion which has to be "the center of our lives." In this way we live a new life with God. The whole purpose of creation is the love of God in our hearts and the beauty of the works of the Holy Spirit in our hearts. We answer to the beauty of God by our own spiritual beauty that we receive from Him. The fruit of God's love is spiritual beauty. Human souls desire the presence of the Holy Spirit. When we have the presence of God in us, we are beautiful in the eyes of God. Like flowers. The desire for God and for His light is very important in our spiritual life:

"Open your hearts to God like the spring flowers which crave for the sun." (January 31, 1985)

Beauty is a fruit of love. Once Jelena asked Our Lady, "How come you are so beautiful?" Our Lady answered:

"I love, that is why I am so beautiful. You also love and you will be beautiful." (March 25, 1985)

We should be a beautiful flower for Jesus and His Mother. Only through prayer can we attain spiritual beauty and complete love:

"Pray, because in prayer each one of you will be able to achieve complete love." (October 25, 1987)

Only through prayer can we be truly beautiful to God:

"When you pray, you are much more beautiful, like flowers, which after the snow, show all their beauty and all their colors become indescribable." **(December 18, 1986)**

With our lives united with God, we can truly discover the real life that God wants to unveil to us. The gift of life is in itself something marvelous. The intensity of life with God is a gift that comes from love. Life must be a joy, a discovery of joy. But that intense life which is a discovery of joy can only exist in God:

"See, little children, how nature opens itself and gives life and fruit. In the same manner I call you also to life with God and abandon yourselves completely to Him." **(May 25, 1989)**

A life with God is a discovery of the profoundness of the mystery of life:

"Little children, I am with you and unceasingly I want to lead you into the joy of life." **(May 25, 1989)**

But real joy and the reality of life are only found in God, in union with Him:

"I would like each one of you to discover the joy and the love that exist only in God and that only God can give." **(May 25, 1989)**

But this discovery can happen only with God, through prayer:

"Pray to discover the greatness and the beauty of life that God gives you." **(May 25, 1989)**

Life in abundance and joy are, like beauty, the very fruits of our love toward God and our neighbor. A great call of Our Lady is to rejoice in the life we have received from God:

"Today I invite you all to rejoice in the life which God gives you." **(August 25, 1988)**

The mystery of life reveals itself to us in prayer and thanks to our love:

> **"Little children, rejoice in God the Creator because He has created you so wonderfully."** (August 25, 1988)

If we can really discover <u>true life</u>, we will have an immense joy. And we will give this life and this joy to others in our mission of witnessing to the world. But we have to thank God always in return for everything we receive:

> **"Pray that your life be a joyful thanksgiving, which flows out of your heart like a river of joy."** (August 25, 1988)

This river of joy will be the salvation of the world, because this joy is from God, through the Holy Spirit:

> **"Joy will manifest in your hearts and thus you shall be joyful witnesses of that which My Son and I want from each one of you."** (February 25, 1987)

This world wants joy and satisfaction, but without Jesus and with sin:

> **"Some don't even want to hear about Jesus, but they still want peace and satisfaction."** (July 30, 1987)

> **"I want each one of you to be happy, but with sin nobody can be happy."** (February 25, 1987)

Our Lady wants our happiness, a lasting and eternal happiness, and that begins right here on this earth:

> **"I want each one of you to be happy here on earth and to be with me in Heaven. That is, dear children, the purpose of my coming here and it's my desire."** (May 25, 1987)

The apparitions are to save us, to bring us to Heaven. Heaven can start right here on this earth if we live what Our Lady asks. From day to day we have to prepare ourselves to be closer and closer to God, ready to receive His gifts, to **"become more beautiful."** (October 24, 1985)

Usually, what we need first is to open our intelligence through prayer to understand all this. We are not aware of things of the spiritual life. We have to pray to the Holy Spirit to understand what is going on:

> **"You are not conscious of the messages which God is sending you through me. He is giving you great graces and you do not comprehend them. Pray to the Holy Spirit for enlightenment."** (November 8, 1984)

We are called to holiness in Medjugorje. Our Lady gives us Her great love. This is, once again, the meaning and the reason for the apparitions:

> **"This long time that I am with you is a sign that I love you immeasurably and that I want each individual to become holy.** (October 9, 1986)

But Satan wants to stop us on the way of holiness:

> **"Satan is strong . . . . Pray, and that way he will neither be able to injure you nor block you on the way of holiness."** (September 25, 1987)

Let us pray that no one would be afraid of holiness; this is not something out of our reach. This is a gift that will be given to us if we humbly live the messages. All we have to think about is how to live the messages. Then the Holy Spirit will do the work in us; we are not going to be saints through our own will power. Holiness is a gift from Heaven, just as the apparitions are a gift from Heaven.

CHAPTER 10

CONCLUSION

Each message added to the other during the years create a mosaic. If we casually read one message taken out of the context of all the rest of the messages, the message on its own may seem simplistic and dull. Similarly, a colored stone removed from a mosaic would seem to have no value by itself; but if we see the whole picture, we have a rich and beautiful picture. We have to see the whole picture:

"By means of the messages, I wish to make a very beautiful mosaic in your hearts." (November 25, 1989)

The whole pedagogy (way or technique of teaching) of Our Lady is to walk with us step by step, message by message, to reeducate us to be Christians. Today, a lot of people think it's not important to be a Christian. Other people want to live a traditional and superficial form of Christianity which is actually only a part of a certain social order with which you have to conform. This form of religion is something that makes Our Lady cry; therefore, again, She wants to show us through the messages the real face of Christianity. This is a long process because men went very far away from the truth, both in the Church and outside the Church. We have to accept being totally reeducated, little by little, by the Mother of God. The problem of mankind is not so much that people have bad intentions, we have plenty of good-hearted people around. The only thing is that they don't see the truth; they are in darkness, and many are just blind. They don't realize that they put themselves in the hands of Satan because they do not know how to tell right from wrong. Many become the image of Satan, as we realize when we watch TV these days with all the sex and horror shows, the "heavy metal-music," and the spectacle of crime and death constantly present in our living

rooms through the news media. Even children's movies and shows
are touched by some Satanic influences . . . . We can understand all
that through the messages:

> **"Darkness reigns over the whole world."** (July 30, 1987)

> **"This unfaithful world walking in darkness . . ."** (June 5,
> 1986)

> **"You are ready to commit sin, and to put yourselves in the
> hands of Satan without reflecting."** (May 25, 1987)

> **"Do not allow Satan to get control of your hearts, so you
> would be an image of Satan and not of me."** (January 30,
> 1986)

If we want a general description of the beautiful mosaic of the
messages, what would we have?

We know about five main messages:

PRAYER   **"Prayer is the only way to save the human race."**
                    (July 30, 1987)

FASTING   **"Repeated prayers and fasting reduce
                    punishments from God."** (November 6, 1982)

BIBLE   **"You have forgotten the Bible,"** said Our Lady,
READING   crying.

CONFESSION   **"Monthly confession will be a remedy for the
                    Church in the West."** (August 6, 1982)

THE   **"The Mass is the most important and the most
EUCHARIST   holy moment in your lives."**

We also know that Our Lady wants each one of us to be a witness of
Her apparitions to save mankind:

"God has chosen each one of you in order to use you in a great plan for the salvation of mankind." (January 25, 1987)

We know that we should seek holiness to fulfill this plan of salvation. Medjugorje is a call to holiness. Our Lady's main objective in Medjugorje is to lead us to holiness:

"Dear children, you know that for your sake I have remained a long time so I might teach you how to make progress on the way to holiness." (January 1, 1987)

By living the messages we are made holy, little by little:

"If you live the messages you are living the seeds of holiness." (October 10, 1985)

Finally, we should know that we should do everything with love, and always place love in the first place:

"Without love you will achieve nothing." (December 13, 1984)

This is an approach to the whole picture, the **"very beautiful mosaic"** (**November 25, 1989**) of the messages of Our Lady, Queen of Peace, in Medjugorje.

PART II

THE MESSAGES
AND RESPONSES
OF OUR LADY

CHAPTER 1

THE EARLY MESSAGES
OF OUR LADY
AND VARIOUS OTHER MESSAGES

(June 24, 1981 to June 25, 1991)

"I AM THE QUEEN OF PEACE." (The Transfiguration,
August 6, 1981)

Since June, 1981, Our Lady's salutation to the visionaries is always,
"Praised be Jesus." The visionaries' answer to this is, "Forever Jesus
and Mary." Mary's parting words were always, **"Go in Peace,"** or **"Go
in the Peace of God."** Sometimes Our Lady adds, **"My dear children,"**
to the salutation or the parting words.

June 24, 1981

The first apparition takes place in the afternoon. It is a silent and
distant white silhouette on the summit of Podbrdo which later would
be called Hill of Apparition or Apparition Mountain. The second
apparition of the day takes place around 6:00 p.m. Ivanka Ivankovic,
Mirjana Dragicevic, and Milka Pavlovic saw Our Lady the first time
She appeared. Later that day Ivan Ivankovic, Vicka Ivankovic, and
Milka, the little sister of Marija, also saw Our Lady.

June 25, 1981

This is the first day the six visionaries, Ivanka Ivankovic, Mirjana
Dragicevic, Vicka Ivankovic, Marija Pavlovic, Ivan Dragicevic, and
Jakov Cola, saw Our Lady or the Gospa on the hill. These six have
become known as and remain "the visionaries." Our Lady said:

"Praised be Jesus!"

Ivanka asked about her mother had who died two months earlier.

"She is happy. She is with me. (Other version: **"She is your angel in Heaven."**)

The visionaries asked if Our Lady would return the next day. Our Lady responded with a nod of the head. Mirjana asked if Our Lady would give them a sign so that others would believe them. Mirjana believed she had received a sign when the Gospa smiled. Also, Mirjana noticed that her watch had changed time during the apparition. The time went backwards.

"Good-bye, my angels. Go in the peace of God."

June 26, 1981

A crowd of nearly three thousand people were drawn to Apparition Mountain by the luminary signs coming from the hill. Holy water is sprinkled on Our Lady by Vicka. She asks Our Lady to stay if She is indeed the Virgin Mary. Our Lady smiles in response. Ivanka then asked why Our Lady is here and what does She want from the people. Our Lady responded:

"I have come because there are many true believers here. I wish to be with you to convert and to reconcile the whole world."

Ivanka asked if her mother has any message for her.

"Obey your grandmother and help her because she is old."

Mirjana wanted to know about her grandfather who had recently died.

"He is well."

The visionaries requested a sign for those who don't see Our Lady to prove that the apparition was really the Gospa.

"Blessed are those who have not seen and who believe."

Mirjana asked: "Who are you?"

"I am the Blessed Virgin Mary."

More questions from the visionaries: "Why are you appearing to us? We are no better than others."

"I do not necessarily choose the best."

"Will you come back?"

"Yes, to the same place as yesterday."

While Marija goes down the mountain, she is mysteriously pushed to the side of the trail by an unseen force. She sees the Virgin again. Our Lady is crying and there is a bare wooden cross behind Her.

"Peace, Peace, Peace! Be reconciled! Only Peace. Make your peace with God and among yourselves. For that, it is necessary to believe, to pray, to fast, and to go to confession."

June 27, 1981

"Praised be Jesus!"

Jakov wanted to know what the Virgin expected of the Franciscans in Medjugorje.

"Have them persevere in the faith and protect the faith of the people."

Mirjana and Jakov were concerned because the people were treating them like liars. They asked Our Lady to leave a sign for the people.

"My angels, do not be afraid of injustices. They have always existed."

The visionaries asked: "How must we pray?"

"Continue to recite The Lord's Prayer, the Hail Mary, and the Glory Be seven times, but also add the Creed. Good-bye, my angels. Go in the peace of God."

Our Lady said to Ivan:

"Be in peace and take courage."

June 28, 1981

The visionaries want to know what the Gospa wishes.

"That people believe and persevere in the faith."

Vicka asked: "What do you expect from the priests?"

"That they remain strong in the faith and that they help you."

They asked Our Lady why She does not appear to everyone in the church.

"Blessed are they who believe without having seen."

They wanted to know if She would return.

"Yes, to the same place."

The visionaries ask if She prefers prayer or singing.

"Both, prayer and singing."

Vicka asked what Our Lady wished from the crowd gathered on the hill. According to the visionaries, Our Lady responded with a smile and a loving glance. At this point, the Gospa disappeared. The visionaries prayed, hoping She would return because She had not told them good-bye. It was during the song, "You Are All Beautiful," that She returned.

Three times Vicka asked, "Dear Gospa (Croatian word for Our Lady), what do you expect of these people?"

"That those who do not see believe as those who see."

Once again the visionaries asked for a sign so that the people would not think of them as liars. They only received a smile from Our Lady as She told them good-bye and disappeared.

"Go in the peace of God."

June 29, 1981

The visionaries wanted to know if the Gospa was happy to see so many people present.

"More than happy."

They ask, "How long will You stay?"

"As long as you will want me to, my angels."

They questioned Our Lady about Her expectations about those who came despite the heat and the brambles.

"There is only one God, one faith. Let the people believe firmly and do not fear anything."

"What do you expect of us?" the visionaries inquired.

"That you have a solid faith and that you maintain confidence."

The visionaries wanted to know if they would be strong enough to endure persecutions because of their beliefs.

"You will be able to, my angels. Do not fear. You will be able to endure everything. You must believe and have confidence in me."

At this point, Doctor Darinka Glamuzina, working for the Government, requests Vicka to ask a question for her: "May I touch Our Lady?"

"There have always been Judases who don't believe, but she can approach."

Vicka shows Doctor Glamuzina where to extend her hand and Doctor Glamuzina touches the Gospa.

The parents of a handicapped child ask the visionaries to intercede on behalf of the child. They ask the Virgin to cure the child so that people will believe them.

"Have them believe strongly in his cure. Go in the peace of God."

The child was cured later that same evening.

Between June 30, 1981 and December 31, 1981, visionaries were being tracked down by the police. They had to find a discreet place to wait for the Virgin to appear.

June 30, 1981

Two social workers took the visionaries on a ride so they would miss the apparition on the hill. The apparition took place at Cerno, on the road between Ljbuski and Medjugorje. Mirjana asked Our Lady if She was angry because they were not on the hill. Our Lady responded:

"That doesn't matter."

Mirjana then asked if Our Lady would be angry if they did not return to the hill, but waited for the apparitions at the church. Somehow Our Lady seemed undecided (according to Mirjana), but then She agreed to appear in the Church and added:

"Always at the same time. Go in the peace of God."

Mirjana, who had been reading an account of the apparitions at Lourdes, thought she understood that the Virgin would return for another three days, until Friday, as She had in Lourdes. However, this was only Mirjana's interpretation.

June, 1981

"I invite you. I need you. I chose you. You are important."

July 1, 1981

Again the visionaries ask the Gospa for a sign. Our Lady appeared to nod her head.

"Good-bye, my dear angels."

July 21, 1981

Our Lady arrived:

"Praised be Jesus."

The visionaries asked again for a sign and the Gospa said yes. They asked how long She would continue to visit them.

"My sweet angels, even if I were to leave the sign, many people will not believe. Many people will only come here and bow down, but people must be converted and do penance."

The visionaries asked the Virgin about the sick and She said they would find the cure in strong faith. The Gospa then departed:

"Go in the peace of God."

July 22, 1981

"Praised be Jesus Christ. A good many people have been converted and among them some had not gone to Confession in 45 years, and now they are going to Confession. Go in the peace of God."

July 23, 1981

"Praised be Jesus Christ."

July 24, 1981

Again the visionaries asked questions concerning the sick.

"Without faith, nothing is possible. All those who will believe firmly will be cured."

July 25, 1981

After more questions about the sick, Our Lady answered:

"God, help us all!"

July 27, 1981

The visionaries ask the Virgin to bless some objects.

"In the name of the Father, and of the Son, and of the Holy Spirit."

Once again the visionaries asked about the sign.

"Wait, it will be soon."

Vicka asked to see Our Lady again this evening and She said:

"I will appear to you again at 11:15 p.m. Go in the peace of God."

As Our Lady was ascending back to heaven the visionaries saw the heart and the cross. Our Lady said:

"My angels, I send you my Son, Jesus, Who was tortured for His faith, and yet He endured everything. You also, my angels, will endure everything."

They see Jesus's head, brown eyes, beard, and long hair to prepare them for the suffering and persecution they were having to endure.

The visionaries are praised for their beautiful singing and praying.

"It is beautiful to listen to you. Continue in this manner. Don't be afraid for Jozo." [He was threatened by the police.]

July 29, 1981

The Virgin appeared in Vicka's room. They asked about a sick person.

"Praised be Jesus! She will be cured. She must believe firmly."

The visionaries asked to embrace Our Lady.

"Yes. Go in the peace of God."

July, 1981

"Carry out well your responsibilities and what the Church asks you to do."

Early August, 1981

The visionaries asked what Our Lady wanted of them later on in life.

"It would be good if you become priests and religious, but only if you, yourselves, would want it. It is up to you to decide."

August 2, 1981

From Marija's room, Our Lady asks her and 40 others:

"All of you together go to the meadow at Gumno. A great struggle is about to unfold. A struggle between my Son and Satan. Human souls are at stake."

[At Gumno] **"Everyone here may touch me."** [When Our Lady's dress became stained, Marinko invited all to go to Confession.]

August 6, 1981 (THE TRANSFIGURATION)

"I am the Queen of Peace."

August 7, 1981

Our Lady asked the young people to come to Cross Mountain at 2:00 a.m. and to pray that many people would do penance for sinners.

"That one do penance for sins."

August 8, 1981

"Do penance! Strengthen your faith through prayer and the sacraments."

August 17, 1981

"Do not be afraid. I wish that you would be filled with joy and that the joy could be seen on your face. I will protect Father Jozo." [The pastor was put in jail.]

August 22, 1981

"Father Jozo has nothing to fear. All troubles will pass."

August 23, 1981

"Praised be Jesus! I have been with Ivan until now. Pray, my angels, for these people. My children, I give you strength. I will always give it to you. When you need me, call me."

August 25, 1981

Some of the people present asked to touch the Virgin.

"It is not necessary to touch me. Many are those who do not feel anything when they touch me. On the matter of the sign, you do not have to become impatient for the day will come."

Our Lady also said there was a spy among those gathered.

August 26, 1981

Because the visionaries see Our Lady, many have been seeking their advice. Our Lady responds:

"Praised be Jesus. Do not give advice to anyone. I know what you feel and that will pass, also."

August 27, 1981

On this day the visionaries again asked something regarding the sign.

"Very soon, I promise you. Be strong and courageous."

August 28, 1981

The visionaries have been waiting for the Virgin in Father Jozo's room. She does not come. This is the second time this has happened. The visionaries go to church to pray and Our Lady appears to them there.

"I was with Father Jozo. That is why I did not come. Do not trouble yourselves if I do not come. It suffices then to pray."

Today Ivan entered the seminary at Visoko. Our Lady told him:

"You are very tired. Rest, so that you can find strength. Go in the peace of God. Good-bye."

August 29, 1981

Jakov asks Our Lady several questions. "Are you also appearing to Ivan in the seminary?"

"Yes, just like for you."

"Is Ivan Ivankovic [who is in prison] well?"

"He is well. He is enduring everything. All will pass. Father Jozo sends you greetings."

Ivan at the Seminary wants to know about the village.

"My angels perform their penance well.

Ivan asked Our Lady whether She was going to help him and his friends in school.

"God's help manifests itself everywhere.

"Go in the peace of God with the blessing of Jesus and mine. Good-bye."

Ivanka asks if a sign will be left soon.

"Again, a little patience."

August 30, 1981

Our Lady arrived and Vicka asks for confirmation about rumors that Father Jozo's cell doors unlock themselves.

"Praised be Jesus! It is true, but no one believes it."

Ivanka asked about Mirjana.

"Mirjana is sad because she is all alone. I will show her to you."

And the visionaries saw Mirjana crying.

Regarding young people who betray the Faith:

"Yes, there are many."

Regarding a woman who wants to leave her husband because he is cruel to her:

"Let her remain close to him and accept her suffering. Jesus, Himself, also suffered."

Regarding a sick young boy:

"He is suffering from a very grave illness. Let his parents firmly believe, do penance, then the little boy will be cured."

Jakov asks about the sign.

"Again, a little patience."

Ivan wants to know how he will do in seminary.

"Be without fear. I am close to you everywhere and at all times."

Ivan asks if the people in his village are pious.

"Your village has become the most fervent parish in Hercegovina. A large number of people distinguish themselves by their piety and their faith."

End of August, 1981

The visionaries asked which is the best form of fasting.

"A fast on bread and water.

"I am the Queen of Peace."

September 1, 1981

The visionaries ask if there will be a Mass on Mt. Krizevac.

"Yes, my angels."

Jacov asks if a trap is being set around the church.

"There's nothing at all. Have the people pray and remain in church as long as possible."

Ivan prayed with Our Lady so that Jesus would help him in his vocation. Our Lady said:

"Go in the peace of God. Do not be afraid. I am close to you and I watch over you."

September 2, 1981

Vicka asked about a young person who hanged himself.

"Satan took hold of him. This young man should not have done that. The Devil tries to reign over the people. He takes everything into his hands, but the force of God is more powerful, and God will conquer."

Ivan wants to know how his friends and he will do in the seminary.

"You are, and you will always be my children. You have followed the path of Jesus. No one will stop you from propagating the faith in Jesus. One must believe strongly."

September 3, 1981

Jakov asked when the sign would be announced.

"Again, a little patience."

September 4, 1981

Ivanka and Marija are concerned that they will not have enough time to pray because they are only home on Saturdays and Sundays and far away at school during the week. (Marija stays in Mostar with relatives.)

"It is enough for you to pray. Come here on Saturdays and
Sundays. I will appear to all of you."

Ivan asks when Our Lady will leave the sign.

"The sign will be given at the end of the apparitions."

Ivan inquires when that will be.

"You are impatient, my angels. Go in the peace of God."

September 5, 1981

"Praised be Jesus and Mary. Go in the peace of God, my
angel. May the blessing of God accompany you. Amen.
Good-bye*."

* Word by word: "Go with God" or "With God" as in the French
"Adieu."

September 6, 1981

"Pray especially on Sunday, so that the great sign, the gift of
God may come. Pray with fervor and a constancy so that God
may have mercy on His great children. Go in peace, my angel.
May the blessing of God accompany you. Amen. Good-bye."

September 7, 1981

"Be converted all of you who are still there. The sign will come
when you will be converted."

September 8, 1981
(FEAST OF THE NATIVITY OF THE VIRGIN)

"I ask you only to pray with fervor. Prayer must become a
part of your daily life to permit the true faith to take root."

Jakov wishes Our Lady a happy birthday.

**"For me it is a beautiful day. With respect to you, persevere
in the faith and in prayer. Do not be afraid. Remain in joy.
It is my desire. Let joy appear on your faces. I will continue
to protect Father Jozo."**

September 10, 1981

Ivan reports that after praying beautiful prayers with a feeling from
the heart filled with love and joy Our Lady says:

"Go in the peace of God, my angel. Amen. Good-bye."

September 13, 1981

The Virgin came near the image of Jesus after some seminary
students came from Confession.

**"This is your Father*, my angel. Go in the peace of God, my
angels."**

* Many known mystics referred, of course, to Jesus as our Brother
but in some rare occasions also as a Father. This is theologically
right, if unusual.

September 14, 1981

Our Lady told Vicka:

**"Stay here so that Jakov will not be alone. Persevere, both of
you, with patience. You will be rewarded."**

September 15, 1981

**"If the people are not converted very soon, bad things will
happen to them."**

September 16, 1981

> "The militia will not stay here a long time. I will leave the
> sign. Be patient still. Don't pray for yourselves. You have
> been rewarded. Pray for others."

September 17, 1981

Concerning someone ill.

> "He will die very soon."

To the visionaries:

> "Persevere and you will be rewarded."

September 20, 1981

To Vicka and Jakov:

> "Do not be lax in your prayers. I ask both of you to fast for a
> week on bread and water."

September 30, 1981

To Vicka and Jakov:

> "Don't ask useless questions dictated by curiosity. The most
> important thing is to pray, my angels."

October 1, 1981

Are all religions good?

> "Members of all faiths are equal before God. God rules over
> each faith just like a sovereign over his kingdom. In the
> world, all religions are not the same because all people have

**not complied with the commandments of God. They reject and
disparage them."**

Are all Churches the same?

**"In some, the strength of prayer to God is greater, in others,
smaller. That depends on the priests who motivate others to
pray. It depends also on the power which they have."**

Why do You appear to us so often and to others who do not follow
God's path?(*)

**"I appear to you often and in every place. To others, I appear
from time to time and briefly. They do not yet follow the way
of God completely. They are not aware of the gift which He
has made them. That, no one deserves. With time, they also
will come to follow the right way."**

(*) This must be about other apparitions in Hercegovina.

October 6, 1981

**"The evening Mass must be kept permanently. The Mass of
the sick must be celebrated on a specific day, at a time which
is most convenient. Father Tomislav must begin with the
prayer group. It is very necessary. Have Father Tomislav
pray with fervor."**

October 7, 1981

In answer to the question whether there are other intermediaries,
besides Jesus, between God and man:

**"There is only one mediator between God and man, and it is
Jesus Christ."**

In answer to Father Tomislav regarding founding a community like that of Saint Francis of Assisi:

> "God has chosen Saint Francis as His elected one. It would be good to imitate his life. In the meantime, we must realize what God orders us to do."

October 8, 1981

Our Lady has scolded Marija about missing Mass and staying with her friends.

> "You would have done better to attend Mass rather than to satisfy human curiosity."

October 10, 1981

> "It is up to you to pray and to persevere. I have made promises to you; also be without anxiety. Faith will not know how to be alive without prayer. Pray more."

October 11, 1981

The visionaries ask about an old man who disappeared.

> "Tomo Lovic is dead."

October 12, 1981

Where is Paradise and the Kingdom of God?

> "In Heaven."

Our Lady is asked if She is the Mother of God and if She went to heaven before or after Her death.

"I am the Mother of God and the Queen of Peace. I went to
Heaven before death."

When will the sign be left?

"I will not yet leave the sign. I shall continue to appear.
Father Jozo sends you greetings. He is experiencing
difficulties, but he will resist, because he knows why he is
suffering."

October 17, 1981

On the sign:

"It is mine to realize the promise. With respect to the
faithful, have them pray and believe firmly."

October 19, 1981

"Pray for Father Jozo and fast tomorrow on bread and water.
Then you will fast for a whole week on bread and water. Pray,
my angels. Now I will show you Father Jozo."

She shows them a vision of Father Jozo in prison and tells them not
to fear for him because everything will work out fine.

On Marinko, the man who protected the visionaries:

"There are a few similar faithful. He's made a sufficient
number of sacrifices for Jozo. He underwent many torments
and sufferings."

To Marinko personally:

"Continue, and do not let anyone take the faith away from
you."

October 20, 1981

Vicka asked Our Lady to intercede for Father Jozo during his trial
and even to strike someone to stop the trial. Our Lady sings "Jesus
Christ, in Your Name" [sung to the tune of "The Battle Hymn of the
Republic"] with the visionaries. After the song was completed, Our
Lady said:

"Go in the peace of God."

October 21, 1981

Because Vicka is concerned about Fr. Jozo's sentencing and knows
that Our Lady is not motivated by vengeance, she begs Her to
intercede that the people involved be reasonable and impartial.

**"Jozo looks well and he greets you warmly. Do not fear for
Jozo. He is a saint. I have already told you. Sentence will not
be pronounced this evening. Do not be afraid, he will not be
condemned to a severe punishment. Pray only, because Jozo
asks from you prayer and perseverance. Do not be afraid
because I am with you."**

October 22, 1981

"Jozo has been sentenced. Let us go to church to pray."

The visionaries tell Our Lady they are saddened because of Father
Jozo.

"You should rejoice!"

The visionaries ask if the whiteness of the cross is a supernatural
phenomenon.

"Yes, I confirm it."

Many saw the cross transform itself into a light and then into a silhouette of Our Lady.

"All of these signs are designed to strengthen your faith until I leave you the visible and permanent sign."

October 25, 1981

The visionaries asked Our Lady about the great light three girls saw on their way home from Mass. Within the light, they saw fifteen figures.

"It was a supernatural phenomenon. I was among the saints."

October 26, 1981

"Praised be Jesus. You are not to ask me any more questions on the subject of the sign. Do not be afraid, it will surely appear. I carry out my promises. As far as you are concerned, pray, persevere in prayer."

October 28, 1981

The visionaries ask if the Gospa appeared at Krizevac the day before for thirty minutes.

"Yes, didn't you see me?"

Regarding the fire that hundreds of people saw that burned but did not consume anything:

"The fire, seen by the faithful, was of a supernatural character. It is one of the signs, a forerunner of the great sign."

October 29, 1981

> "You, my angels, be on your guard. There is enough mendacious news which people are spreading. Of course, I will show you my mercy. Be a little patient. Pray!"

October 30, 1981

> "Praised be Jesus!"

Jakov and Vicka questioned Our Lady about a sealed envelop which an official showed them wishing to trick them.

> "Do not respond anything. It is a bad trick which they are playing on you. They have already given so much false news. Do not believe them. Continue to pray and to suffer! I will make the power of love appear."

The visionaries asked Our Lady when should Christmas Mass be celebrated.

> "Have them celebrate it at midnight. Pray! Go in the peace of God!"

To Ivanka:

> "Pray more. The others are praying and suffering more than you."

To the visionaries:

> "Tell the young people not to allow themselves to be distracted from the true way. Let them remain faithful to their religion."

October 31, 1981

From Vicka's diary we learn that Mirjana has had daily apparitions in Sarajevo where she is a student at a professional school. Our Lady counsels Mirjana as a wise mother would, telling her two times who to trust, who to distrust, and how to respond to those who rebuke her and attack God.

Our Lady knows and advised Mirjana to avoid a friend who wants to get her involved with drugs. Our Lady suggested that she answer questions when that would be helpful and to remain quiet when that would be more beneficial. Our Lady shared Her joy over the five visionaries being together and tells them that Father Jozo would not be in prison more than four years.

Regarding Danny Ljolje, Our Lady said:

"There is a lot of deception and erroneous information."

After showing the visionaries a part of paradise and telling them not to be afraid, Our Lady said:

"All those who are faithful to God will have that."

October, 1981

Concerning the conflict between the Franciscans and the Bishop of Mostar:

"It is going to find a solution. We must have patience and pray."

Regarding Poland:

"There will be great conflicts, but in the end, the just will take over."

Regarding Russia:

> "The Russian people will be the people who will glorify God the most. Regarding the West: the West has made civilization progress, but without God, as if they were their own creators."

November 1, 1981

> "Be persevering! Pray! Many people are beginning to convert."

November 2, 1981

The visionaries questioned the Gospa about Her reasons for showing them paradise some days earlier.

> "I did it so that you could see the happiness which awaits those who love God."

Jesus then appears to them with injuries covering His body and wearing a crown of thorns.

> "Do not be afraid. It is my Son. See how He has been martyred. In spite of all, He was joyful and He endured all with patience."

Then Jesus says:

> "Look at me. How I have been injured and martyred! In spite of all, I have gained the victory. You also, my angels, be persevering in your faith and pray so that you may overcome."

November 3, 1981

The song, 'Come, Come to Us Lord,' was begun by Our Lady and the visionaries joined in with Her.

"I am often at Krizevac, at the foot of the cross, to pray there. Now I pray to my Son to forgive the world its sins. The world has begun to convert."

November 6, 1981

During this apparition, Our Lady disappears and the visionaries see a terrifying, horrendous vision of Hell. Then Our Lady reappears and says:

"Do not be afraid! I have shown you Hell so that you may know the state of those who are there."

November 8, 1981

Our Lady appears kissing and lovingly embracing a picture of John Paul II.

"He is your father, the spiritual father of all. It is necessary to pray for him."

One account tells of Our Lady picking up the picture in the room.

The visionaries have a vision of Father Jozo in prison.

"Have you seen how our Father Jozo struggles for God?"

November 9, 1981

The militia passes by the room where Our Lady was about to appear.

"Do not be afraid of the militia. Do not provoke anybody. Be polite with everybody."

November 10, 1981

> **"Do not give in. Keep your faith. I will accompany you at
> every step."**

November 13, 1981

> **"Praised be Jesus!"**

Our Lady showed the visionaries a beautiful landscape with the Baby
Jesus walking there. The visionaries were not able to recognize Him.
Emphasizing the song She sang during the November 3, 1981
apparition.

> **"It is Jesus. On my arrival and when I depart, always sing the
> song, 'Come, Come to us O Lord.'"**

November 15, 1981

This apparition was to take place in Fr. Jozo's room but Our Lady
appeared later in the Church and said someone had placed (hidden)
listening devices in the room. She relates:

> **"The world is on the point of receiving great favors from me
> and my Son. May the world keep a strong confidence."**

November 16, 1981

> **"The Devil is trying to conquer us. Do not permit him. Keep
> the faith, fast, and pray. I will be with you at every step."**

Her words to Vicka and Jakov:

> **"Persevere with confidence in prayer and in faith."**

November 22, 1981

The Gospa explains the cross, the heart, and the sun to the visionaries.

"These are the signs of salvation: The cross is a sign of mercy, just like the heart. The sun is the source of light, which enlightens us."

Again a shining silhouette takes the place of the cross on Krizevac. The visionaries asked the Blessed Virgin if it was She.

"Why do you ask me, my angels? Have you not seen me? The world must find salvation while there is time. Let it pray with fervor. May it have the spirit of faith."

November 23, 1981

Our Lady was indescribable and beautiful light radiated, flowed, shined, and sparkled around Her.

"The people have begun to convert. Keep a solid faith. I need your prayers."

November 26, 1981

The visionaries asked the Gospa questions about the sick.

"Have strong faith, pray, and fast and they will be cured. Be confident and rest in joy. Go in the peace of God. Be patient and pray for the cure. Good-bye, my dear angels."

November 28, 1981

All but Ivan were present. The visionary, Vicka, relates, "We all felt a profound peace about and within us. Our Lady looked at us with a beautiful sweetness."

"Ah, it is so beautiful to see all of you together! Go in the peace of God, my angels. Good-bye."

November 29, 1981

"It is necessary for the world to be saved while there is still time, for it to pray strongly, and for it to have the spirit of faith."

November, 1981

Vicka warns that this message is not just for the visionaries but for all.

"The Devil tries to impose his power on you, but you must remain strong and persevere in your faith. You must pray and fast. I will always be close to you."

December 2, 1981

The visionaries asked about a young man who had suddenly had a memory loss and could no longer learn anything.

"It is necessary to hospitalize him."

The visionaries asked more questions.

"It is not necessary to ask questions on every subject."

December 3, 1981

"Pray and persevere through prayer."

December 6, 1981

"Be strong and persevering. My dear angels, go in the peace of God."

December 7, 1981

Our Lady looked at the crowds of people.

> **"The people are converting. It is true, but not yet all. Pray
> and persist in prayers."**

After an apparition at Jakov's home, the letters "MIR LJUDIMA"
(Peace to the people) were on the wall in gold.

December 8, 1981
(FEAST OF THE IMMACULATE CONCEPTION)

Our Lady answers the questions the visionaries have about their
futures.

> **"It would be good if all of you become priests and religious,
> but only if you desire it. You are free. It is up to you to
> choose. If you are experiencing difficulties or if you need
> something, come to me. If you do not have the strength to fast
> on bread and water, you can give up a number of things. It
> would be a good thing to give up television, because after
> seeing some programs, you are distracted and unable to pray.
> You can give up alcohol, cigarettes, and other pleasures. You
> yourselves know what you have to do."**

Our Lady then profoundly kneels down, serious with Her hands
extended. She prays to Jesus:

> **"My beloved Son, I beseech you to be willing to forgive the
> world its great sin through which it offends you."**

December 9, 1981

While we were praying, Our Lady intervened:

"Oh, My Son Jesus, forgive these sins; there are so many of them!"

We stopped and became silent.

"Continue to pray, because prayer is the salvation of the people."

December 11, 1981

Vicka asked the Gospa to look after her parents in Germany.

"I promise to protect them. Everything will go well."

December 12, 1981

Our Lady told the visionaries She was happy because they would all be together during vacation.

"Very soon you will all be united. You will be able to have a beautiful time together."

December 16, 1981

"Kneel down, my children, and pray."

December 18, 1981

Our Lady sings "Jesus Christ In Your Name" and says:

"Come on, sing more joyfully. Why are you so pensive?"

She then began the song, "The Queen of the Holy Rosary," before leaving.

December 21, 1981

"Be on your guard, my children. Prepare yourselves for difficult days. All kinds of people will come here."

December 24, 1981

"Celebrate the days which are coming. Rejoice with my Son! Love your neighbor. May harmony reign among you."

December 25, 1981 (CHRISTMAS)

The visionaries see Baby Jesus.

"Love one another, my children. You are brothers and sisters. Don't argue among yourselves. Give glory to God, glorify Him and sing, my angels."

December 30, 1981

Our Lady sings "The Queen of the Holy Rosary."

December 31, 1981

Ivan asked the Gospa how to help doubting priests understand the apparitions.

"It is necessary to tell them that from the very beginning I have been conveying the message of God to the world. It is a great pity not to believe in it. Faith is a vital element, but one cannot compel a person to believe. Faith is the foundation from which everything flows."

Ivan asks Our Lady if it is really She appearing at the foot of the cross.

**"Yes, it is true. Almost everyday I am at the foot of the cross.
My Son carried the cross. He has suffered on the cross, and
by it, He saved the world. Everyday I pray to my Son to forgive
the sins of the world."**

1981

Vicka says that at the very beginning Our Lady told us:

"You may leave, but let little Jakov stay with me."

Vicka then adds that Our Lady thinks that Jakov is a precious boy.

January, 1982 - April 11, 1985

THE APPARITION CHAPEL

In January, the visionaries were moved to a side room to the right of
the Altar of St. James Church. This room was to become famous
and considered by many as sacred ground. Presently, many pilgrims
take great joy in participating at Mass, which is sometimes held in the
"Chapel". Thousands of apparitions took place in the "Chapel" and
one could say Our Lady dwelled there.

January 11, 1982

**"I invite you very specially to participate at Mass. Wait for me
at church, that is the agreeable place."**

January 14, 1982

Today, toward the end of the apparition, two of the visionaries were
reprimanded by Our Lady. The other visionaries could not hear this
correction for their behavior but Our Lady's expression gave them an
indication what it was about. Those reprimanded later said that Our
Lady was kind and respectful to them.

January 18, 1982

Concerning a sick person with heart problems:

"There is little hope for her. I will pray for her."

January 20, 1982

The visionaries want to know if they should meet with children from Izbicno who are also visionaries. They tell the Blessed Virgin that the Izbicno children said She told them about this meeting.

"It is not necessary for you to meet them."

The officials want to transfer Father Tomislav.

"If it is in God's design that he (Father Tomislav) depart as has been the case with Father Jozo, have him abandon himself to the will of God. He must think very much and you must pray for him."

January 21, 1982

Again the visionaries asked about the sign.

"The sign will appear at the desired time."

Our Lady is also asked why apparitions occur at different places in Hercegovina.

"My children, don't you see that the faith begins to extinguish itself and that it is necessary to awaken the faith among men?"

The visionaries want to know what to do to stop quarrels among priests.

"Fast and pray!"

January 22, 1982

Concerning apparitions at Izbicno.

"They are coming from God."

Izbicno is 60 kilometers from Medjugorje. Eighteen people, mostly females, said they are having apparitions between 1982 and 1983.

February 2, 1982

Our Lady was asked when She would like the Feast of The Queen of Peace to be celebrated. She smiled and said:

"I would prefer that it take place June 25th. The faithful have come for the first time on that day, on the hill."

February 8, 1982

The visionaries asked about an emotionally sick person.

"He must pray. I will help him within the limitation of my power."

To some Slovenes who were praying during the apparition:

"Persevere in prayer."

February 9, 1982

"Pray for the sick. Believe firmly. I will come to help, according to that which is in my power. I will ask my Son, Jesus, to help them. The most important thing, in the meantime, is a strong faith. Numerous sick persons think that it is sufficient to come here in order to be quickly healed. Some of them do not even believe in God and even less in the apparitions, and then they ask for help from the Gospa!"

February 10, 1982

Jakov and Vicka ask Our Lady many questions and She answers them. They relate that Our Lady loves the Creed and prefers it to other prayers. They say they have never seen Her happier than during this prayer. Our Lady's message:

"Pray, pray! It is necessary to believe firmly, to go to confession regularly, and likewise to receive Holy Communion. It is the only salvation."

February 11, 1982

"Pray my angels, persevere! Do not let the enemy take possession of you in anything. Be courageous. Go in the peace of God, my angels. Good-bye."

February 12, 1982

"Be more calm, more poised. Do not take sides with other children. Be agreeable, well mannered, pious!"

The visionaries relate that Our Lady prays with Her hands folded and when She speaks, She spreads them, Her palms turned upwards.

February 13, 1982

For seminarians attending the apparition:

"Through prayer, one obtains everything."

February 14, 1982

The visionaries are happy because four of them are together.

"Be together like brothers and sisters. Do not argue. Satan exists! He seeks only to destroy. With regard to you, pray

and persevere in prayer. No one will be able to do anything against you."

February 16, 1982

Vicka relates she has never seen Our Lady sad. Her countenance is always smiling, joyful, and serene. It attracts us and inspires us to be the same way.

"Satan only says what he wants. He interferes in everything. You, my angels, be ready to endure everything. Here, many things will take place. Do not allow yourselves to be surprised by him."

February 19, 1982

Vicka's diary states that the visionaries ask Our Lady if they could pray the Hail Mary and She says yes. Our Lady smiled as they prayed but did not pray with them. Vicka writes that seeing Our Lady, Her beauty, is indescribable and she would do whatever She asks.

"Listen attentively at Holy Mass. Be well mannered. Do not chat during Holy Mass."

February 21, 1982

"Be together, do not argue, and do not be disorderly. My angels, I will make you attentive. I will guide you on a sure way."

February 23, 1982

The visionaries ask if someone is alive.

"Do not ask me any more questions! I know what there is in each sick person or what there is within my power to help him. I will pray to my Son to put out His mercy on each one."

February 25, 1982

"Be persevering and courageous. Do not fear anything. Pray and do not pay attention to others."

Concerning Father Jozo:

"Do not fear for him."

February 28, 1982

"Thank Tomislav very much for he is guiding you very well. Go in the peace of God, my angels!"

March 1, 1982

"All of you, be happy and may my blessing accompany you at each step."

In response to the Yugoslavian authorities' demand that the prayer meetings for the young people end:

"It is better to temporarily suspend prayer meetings and those of meditation because of the authorities. Take them up later, when it will be possible."

March 2, 1982

Smiling at two large pictures of the Pope brought by a woman from Osijek, Our Lady said:

"He is your father, my angels."

Our Lady began The Lord's Prayer, and on leaving said:

> "Open the door well, follow the Mass well! Go in the peace of
> God, my angels! If you suffer for a just cause, blessings will
> be still more abundant for you."

March 4, 1982

Regarding a woman who had no children:

> "Let her believe firmly. God, who comes to help everyone, will
> likewise help her. Be patient, my angels, do not be afraid of
> anything. I am at your side and guard you. If you have any
> problems, whatever it be, call me. I will come immediately and
> help you in advising you on best resolving the difficulty. Go
> in peace, my angels. Good-bye."

March 7, 1982

Regarding Ivan at the Seminary at Visoko:

> "He prays well; he is obedient. He follows my instructions."

March 8, 1982

Regarding a sixteen-year-old boy who had disappeared for a week:

> "He left because of many troubles. He himself created some of
> the problems."

March 9, 1982

Regarding a young man from Hadromilje who disappeared from his
home:

> "He has serious problems. It is necessary to pray for him very
> much, my angels. The people are beginning to be converted.

Prayer has been taken up again in the homes where people
had no longer prayed."

Beginning of April, 1982

Mirjana asked the Blessed Virgin when She would like to be
honored.

"I wish a feast for the Queen of Peace on the 25th of June, the
anniversary of the first apparition."

April 11, 1982 (EASTER SUNDAY)

Concerning the formation of prayer groups:

"It is necessary, but not only here. Communities of prayer are
necessary in all parishes."

April 21, 1982

To a question asked by Father Tomislav Vlasic, Our Lady answers:

"Be patient! Everything is developing according to God's plan.
His promises will be realized. May one continue to pray, to do
penance, and to be converted."

April 22, 1982

Concerning the luminous signs at the cross on Krizevac:

"They are signs of God and not of natural phenomena. 'S' and
'T' are signs of salvation."

"S" stands for salvation. "T" stands for the cross.

April 24, 1982

Concerning what needs to be done in order to have more cures:

"Pray! Pray and believe firmly. Say the prayers which have
already been requested. (The Lord's Prayer, the Hail Mary,
and the Glory Be seven times each, and the Creed.) Do more
penance."

May 2, 1982

"I have come to call the world to conversion for the last time.
Afterwards, I will not appear any more on this earth."

May 6, 1982

Concerning putting the date and description of the sign in a sealed
envelop and putting it in the archives:

"No! I have entrusted that only to you. You will unveil it when
I will tell you. Many persons will not believe you, I know, and
you will suffer very much for it. But you will endure
everything and you will finally be the happiest."

May 13, 1982

Concerning the assassination attempt on the life of John Paul II:

"His enemies have wanted to kill him, but I protected him."

Spring, 1982

The Pastor at Izbicno has the visionaries ask concerning all of the
signs in Hercegovina and Our Lady's appearing in so many places:

"It is God who gives them. My children, have you not
observed that faith began to extinguish itself? There are many

who do not come to church except through habit. It is necessary to awaken the faith. It is a gift from God. If it is necessary, I will appear in each home."

To the visionaries regarding seeing the seers from Izbicno:

"Did I not tell you not to come together with those children? I am your mother, you must obey me."

To Jakov, crying because he saw Vicka ill:

"The cross is necessary because of the sins of the world."

June 23, 1982

Responses from Our Lady regarding questions asked by Father Tomisalv Vlasic. Vicka asked the Gospa the questions for Father Tomisalv. He reported the answers in the parish Chronicle.

1. The most important thing is that you, the visionaries, remain united. Let peace be among you. Pay very close attention to that. Obey and do what the priests and your parents tell you. Go often to Holy Mass and receive Communion. Be very attentive these days. Some dishonest people will come to you, in numbers, in order to tempt you. Be careful of your statements. These days I am expecting of you a very special discipline. Do not move around anywhere, or often, and do not separate from one another.

2. A number of those who have been very enthusiastic will cool off. But you, persist and be proud of each of my words. Have the people pray very much. Have them pray more for salvation and only for salvation, because it is in prayer. And let the people be converted so long as it is possible. There are many sins, vexations, curse words, lies, and other bad things. Let them be converted, go to confession, and receive Holy Communion.

3. **Let them not print books on the apparitions before the anniversary has passed, because that could have some undesirable consequences.**

4. **You have asked me to keep good and faithful priests in this parish who will continue the work. Do not be afraid of anything. This grace must be given to you. From priests, I do not demand anything other than prayer with perseverance and preaching. May they be patient and wait for the promise of God.**

Concerning the number of natures of the Holy Spirit:

5. **He has only one nature, the Divine nature.**

Concerning these apparitions being the last ones on earth:

6. **These apparitions are the last in the world.**

June 24 or 25, 1982 (date not certain)

"**Thank the people in my name for the prayers, the sacrifices, and the (acts of) penance. Have them persevere in prayer, fasting, and conversion and have them wait with patience for the realization of my promise. Everything is unfolding according to God's plan.**"

July 12, 1982

Concerning a third world war:

"**The third world war will not take place.**"

July 21, 1982

Concerning Purgatory:

"There are many souls in Purgatory. There are also persons who have been consecrated to God - some priests, some religious. Pray for their intentions, at least The Lord's Prayer, the Hail Mary, and the Glory Be seven times each, and the Creed. I recommend it to you. There is a large number of souls who have been in Purgatory for a long time because no one prays for them."

Concerning fasting:

"The best fast is on bread and water. Through fasting and prayer, one can stop wars, one can suspend the laws of nature. Charity cannot replace fasting. Those who are not able to fast can sometime replace it with prayer, charity, and a confession; but everyone, except the sick, must fast."

July 24, 1982

"You go to Heaven in full conscience: that which you have now. At the moment of death, you are conscious of the separation of the body and soul. It is false to teach people that you are reborn many times and that you pass to different bodies. One is born only once. The body, drawn from the earth, decomposes after death. It never comes back to life again. Man receives a transfigured body."

Regarding a question asked about being bad all ones life and asking forgiveness:

"Whoever has done very much evil during his life can go straight to Heaven if he confesses, is sorry for what he has done, and receives Communion at the end of his life."

July 25, 1982

Concerning Hell:

"Today many persons go to Hell. God allows His children to
suffer in Hell due to the fact that they have committed grave,
unpardonable sins. Those who are in Hell no longer have a
chance to know a better lot."

Other answers from Our Lady state that people who commit grave
sins live in hell while here on earth and continue this hell in eternity.
They actually go to hell because they chose it in life and at the
moment of death.

Concerning cures:

"For the cure of the sick, it is important to say the following
prayers: the Creed, and seven times each, The Lord's Prayer,
the Hail Mary, and the Glory Be, and to fast on bread and
water. It is good to impose one's hands on the sick and to
pray. It is good to anoint the sick with Holy oil. All priests
do not have the gift of healing. In order to receive this gift,
the priest must pray with perseverance and believe firmly."

August 6, 1982 (THE TRANSFIGURATION)

Concerning Confession:

"One must invite people to go to Confession each month,
especially the first Saturday. Here, I have not spoken about
it yet. I have invited people to frequent Confession. I will
give you yet some concrete messages for our time. Be patient
because the time has not yet come. Do what I have told you.
They are numerous who do not observe it. Monthly
Confession will be a remedy for the Church in the West. One
must convey this message to the West."

That night, after the apparition, two luminary signs in the form of
rays of light were displayed on the Cross at Krizevac and on the
Church. Ivan and a group of young people had been praying on the
hill of Bijakovici. Before the sign appeared, Our Lady said:

"Now I am going to give you a sign in order to strengthen your faith."

Many members of the prayer group saw this sign.

August 10, 1982

Our Lady told the visionaries that priests could give out written information about certain things.

August 11, 1982

The visionaries were scolded by Our Lady for their conduct during the evening Mass. No special message was given.

August 15, 1982

Vicka and Ivanka were given a new secret during the seven-minute apparition. The others could not hear the voice of Our Lady, but they understood that a secret had been given.

August 16, 1982

Our Lady corrected the speed and quality of the prayers of those in Church as well as the visionaries.

During the apparition, Mirjana reports that she sees heavenly persons, such as Jesus, Mary, and angels, in three dimensions (as another human person would be seen), and earthly people in two dimensions (as in a picture or photograph). She saw Father Jozo or Ivan Ivankovic, who have been imprisoned because of their faith, as if in a motion picture and two dimensional.

August 18, 1982

Concerning the sick, Mirjana reports:

"Have them believe and pray; I cannot help him who does not
pray and does not sacrifice. The sick, just like those who are
in good health, must pray and fast for the sick. The more you
believe firmly, the more you pray and fast for the same
intention, the greater is the grace and the mercy of God."

Concerning a planned marriage between a Catholic and an Orthodox:

"In my eyes and in the sight of God, everything is equal. But
for you, it is not the same thing because you are divided. If it
is possible, it is better if she were not to marry this man
because she will suffer and her children also. She will be able
to live and follow only with difficulty, the way of her faith."

August 29, 1982

Concerning reports that the apparitions have divided the priests in
Hercegovina:

"I have not desired your division. On the contrary, I desire
that you be united. Do not ignore the fact that I am the Queen
of Peace. If you desire practical advise: I am the Mother who
has come from the people; I cannot do anything without the
help of God. I, too, must pray like you. It is because of that,
that I can only say to you: Pray, fast, do penance, and help
the weak. I am sorry if my preceding answer was not
agreeable to you. Perhaps you do not want to understand it."

August 31, 1982

"I do not dispose all graces. I receive from God what I obtain
through prayer. God has placed His complete trust in me. I
particularly protect those who have been consecrated to me.
The great sign has been granted. It will appear independently
of the conversion of the people."

September 4, 1982

"Jesus prefers that you address yourselves directly to Him
rather than through an intermediary. In the meantime, if you
wish to give yourselves completely to God and if you wish that
I be your protector, then confide to me all your intentions,
your fasts, and your sacrifices so that I can dispose of them
according to the will of God."

September 26, 1982

Concerning a religious from Rome:

"Have her strengthen the faith of those who have been
entrusted to her."

Concerning Father Robert Faricy and Fr. Forrest:

"They are on the good path. Have them persist."

Concerning the Pope:

"Have him consider himself the father of all mankind and not
only of Christians. Have him spread untiringly and with
courage the message of peace and love among all mankind."

October 1, 1982

"I am happy because you have begun to prepare the monthly
observance of the Sacrament of Reconciliation. That will be
good for the whole world. Persevere in prayer. It is the true
way which leads you toward my Son."

November 4, 1982

Concerning the vision of Andja, from Mostar, of 13 people coming
from the East and on another occasion, six persons:

"It is about a true vision. They were some souls of her close family from Purgatory. It is necessary to pray for them."

November 6, 1982

Concerning the eighth secret, Mirjana is frightened and prays to Our Lady for mercy on mankind:

"I have prayed; the punishment has been softened. Repeated prayers and fasting reduce punishments from God, but it is not possible to avoid entirely the chastisement. Go on the streets of the city, count those who glorify God and those who offend Him. God can no longer endure that."

November 8, 1982

Concerning the necessity of writing to the Bishop and priests about asking the faithful to intensify their prayers or waiting for other events:

"It is better to wait than to precipitate that."

November 15, 1982

Jakov asked Our Lady concerning Vicka's illness and the advisability of her being admitted to a hospital in Zagreb. He asked because Vicka would not ask, desiring to be left to the will of God.

"It is necessary to send Vicka to Zagreb."

December 18, 1982

Concerning responding to the Bishop of Mostar about his article concerning events in Medjugorje:

"Yes, respond!"

December 20, 1982

Concerning the same article, the visionaries wanted to know the necessity of giving objective information to the faithful in Hercegovina.

"No!"

Should the visionaries only pray with Our Lady and the pilgrims ask their questions only to the priests?

"Yes, it is better that the children pray with me and that the pilgrims ask the priests and look for solutions with them. Meanwhile, I will continue to answer the questions which they ask me."

Before December 26, 1982

This is information which Mirjana gave to Father Tomislav Vlasic on November 5, 1983. He conveyed this information to the Pope on December 16, 1983. Father Vlasic's letter was published in Is the Virgin Mary Appearing at Medjugorje? (Paris, 1984), with this introduction:

"During the apparition of December 25, 1982, according to Mirjana, the Madonna confided to her the tenth and last secret, and revealed to her, the dates in which the different secrets will be realized. The Blessed Virgin revealed to Mirjana some aspects of the future, up to this point, in greater detail than to the other seers. For this reason, I am reporting here what Mirjana told me in a conversation of November 5, 1983. I summarized the essentials of her account, without literal quotation. Mirjana told me:

Before the visible sign is given to mankind, there will be three warnings to the world. The warnings will be in the form of events on earth. Mirjana will be a witness to them. Ten days before one of the admonitions, Mirjana will notify a priest of her choice. The witness of Mirjana will be a confirmation of the apparitions and a stimulus for the conversion of the world.

After the admonitions, the visible sign will appear on the site of the apparitions in Medjugorje for all the people to see. The sign will be given as a testimony to the apparitions and in order to call people back to faith.

The ninth and tenth secrets are serious. They concern chastisement for the sins of the world. Punishment is inevitable, for we cannot expect the whole world to be converted. The punishment can be diminished by prayer and penance, but it cannot be eliminated. Mirjana says that one of the evils that threatened the world, the one contained in the seventh secret, has been averted thanks to prayer and fasting. That is why the Blessed Virgin continues to encourage prayer and fasting:

'You have forgotten that through prayer and fasting you can avert wars and suspend the laws of nature.'

After the first admonition, the others will follow in a rather short time. Thus, people will have some time for conversion.

That interval will be a period of grace and conversion. After the visible sign appears, those who are still alive will have little time for conversion. For that reason, the Blessed Virgin invites us to urgent conversion and reconciliation.

The invitation to prayer and penance is meant to avert evil and war, but most of all to save souls.

According to Mirjana, the events predicted by the Blessed Virgin are near. By virtue of this experience, Mirjana proclaims to the world: 'Convert as quickly as possible. Open your hearts to God.'

"In addition to this basic message, Mirjana related an apparition she
had in 1982 which we believe sheds some light on some aspects of
Church history. She spoke of an apparition in which Satan appeared
to her. Satan asked Mirjana to renounce the Madonna and follow
him. That way she could be happy in love and in life. He said that
following the Virgin, on the contrary, would only lead to suffering.
Mirjana rejected him, and immediately the Virgin gave her the
following message, in substance:

'Excuse me for this, but you must realize that Satan exists.
One day he appeared before the throne of God and asked
permission to submit the Church to a period of trial. God
gave him permission to try the Church for one century. This
century is under the power of the Devil, but when the secrets
confided to you come to pass, his power will be destroyed.
Even now he is beginning to lose his power and has become
aggressive. He is destroying marriages, creating division
among priests and is responsible for obsessions and murder.
You must protect yourselves against these things through
fasting and prayer, especially community prayer. Carry
blessed objects with you. Put them in your house, and restore
the use of holy water.'"

December 24, 1982

For Mirjana:

"On Christmas I will appear to you for the last time."

After this apparition, it was apparent to the few people present that
Mirjana was very sad. After a time, her mother asked her what the
matter was. This caused Mirjana to leave the room, crying. After
composing herself, she returned to the room and stated that this was
her next to the last apparition. On Christmas Day Our Lady would
come to her again as a gift but would not be giving her daily
apparitions anymore. Mirjana was given the tenth secret, a

particularly grave one. On her birthday, March 18, for the rest of her life, Our Lady promised to appear to her.

December 25, 1982 (CHRISTMAS)

Our Lady's apparition to Mirjana lasted 45 minutes. Mirjana states that she will always remember these words of Our Lady:

> **"Now you will have to turn to God in the faith like any other person. I will appear to you on the day of your birthday and when you will experience difficulties in life. Mirjana, I have chosen you; I have confided in you everything that is essential. I have also shown you many terrible things. You must now bear it all with courage. Think of Me and think of the tears I must shed for that. You must remain courageous. You have quickly grasped the messages. You must also understand now that I have to go away. Be courageous."**

Mirjana has said that Our Lady prepared her for this meeting for a month. In a motherly manner, Our Lady had explained that her task was accomplished and Mirjana had received sufficient information. While Mirjana felt that her conversations with Our Lady were so necessary for her soul, Our Lady promised that as long as she remained close to God, She would help her and be beside her always, assisting her in her most difficult times. But now she must return to the normal state of each Christian.

This was Mirjana's saddest Christmas ever. This last meeting left her feeling as if she had lost the most beautiful thing in her life. Our Lady knew her pain and was there to cheer her up and to pray with her. Mirjana was asked to sing and praise God. Mirjana prayed the Hail Holy Queen, the prayer she always said when she was alone with Our Lady.

As Our Lady had warned, the first month after this last apparition was most difficult. Mirjana experienced depression, avoided people, and shut herself in her room where she had waited for Our Lady.

She cried and called out to Our Lady and did feel Her presence. She waited for her birthday.

Many who know Mirjana claim that since the apparitions stopped, she has become much more mature in her inner life as well as in her character. Our Lady has been the best of educators.

December 27, 1982

Concerning placing the new statue of Our Lady, Queen of Peace, in the church:

"Yes, you may!"

This statue was sculpted by Vipotnik and painted by Luka Stojaknac and Florijan Mickovic. Luka is Orthodox and working on this statue has been a blessing for him.

December 31, 1982

Concerning the new year:

"Pray as much as possible and fast! You must persevere in prayer and fasting. I wish that the new year will be spent in prayer and penance. Persevere in prayer and in sacrifice and I will protect you and will hear your prayers."

January 1, 1983 (HOLY MARY, MOTHER OF GOD)

Concerning Our Lady's appearances to Mirjana:

"After Christmas, I am no longer appearing to her for the present."

January 5, 1983

Ivan, Jakov, Marija, and Vicka relate the following information to Father Tomislav: Marija has received seven secrets; Vicka has received eight; Jakov, Ivanka, and Ivan have received nine; and Mirjana has received ten. As to how long the apparitions will last or why Our Lady no longer appears to Mirjana after Christmas, we do not know. Our Lady constantly invites us to prayer, fasting, and conversion and she confirms her promises.

Ivan's explanation of why Mirjana has ceased having regular apparitions is that she did not pray enough. He further adds that Our Lady probably did it so Mirjana would learn to pray in faith. (On the contrary, others have interpreted the cessation of the apparitions as a sign of achievement and maturity.)

Regarding the time of the sign, it's month and year, Ivan says: "It is forecasted."

January 7, 1983

The visionaries are invited to record Our Lady's testimony as She begins to tell them her life; but, until they receive Her authorization, they will not be able to make this information public. Jakov will receive information until April; Ivanka, until May 22; and Marija, until July 17. When in Medjugorje, Marija receives an abridged account as most of the week she is attending a school for hairdressers in Mostar. For Vicka, this transmission lasted until April 10, 1985 and filled three notebooks.

January 10, 1983

Mirjana shared with Fr. Tomislav Vlasic that during the year and a half that she had been receiving apparitions, she had experienced the maternal love and intimacy of Our Lady and questioned Her why God could so "mercilessly" send sinners to Hell forever.

"Men who go to Hell no longer want to receive any benefit from
God. They do not repent nor do they cease to revolt and to
blaspheme. They make up their mind to live in Hell and do
not contemplate leaving it.

Regarding Purgatory:

"In Purgatory there are different levels; the lowest is close to
Hell and the highest gradually draws near to Heaven. It is
not on All Souls Day, but at Christmas, that the greatest
number of souls leave Purgatory. There are in Purgatory,
souls who pray ardently to God, but for whom no relative or
friend prays on earth. God makes them benefit from the
prayers of other people. It happens that God permits them to
manifest themselves in different ways, close to their relatives
on earth, in order to remind men of the existence of Purgatory
and to solicit their prayers to come close to God who is just,
but good. The majority of people go to Purgatory. Many go
to Hell. A small number go directly to Heaven."

January 12, 1983

There was present a U.S. television crew that was filming the events
in Medjugorje. Fr. John Bertolucci was the narrator. The name
of the Television program was "The Glory of God." Concerned about
the police and the oppression still going on at that time, they were
worried about getting the film out of the country. They were
delighted and at the same time assured because Our Lady cleverly
used their title in Her answer.

"There will be some difficulties, but it will be for the glory of
God."

April 21, 1983

To the visionaries and especially Jakov concerning behavior during
Mass and around others:

"You must behave well; be pious and set a good example for
the faithful."

April 24, 1983

Message for an Italian doctor:

"I bless him just as [I bless] those who work with him at the
hospital in Milan, for everything they are doing. Have them
continue, and pray. I bless the sick of this hospital, just as the
sick for whom you have prayed this evening, and those for
whom you will pray."

June 1, 1983

"Dear children! I hoped that the world would begin to be
converted on its own. Do now everything you can so that the
world can be converted."

June 2, 1983

"Read what has been written about Jesus. Meditate on it and
convey it to others."

June 3, 1983

Concerning Father Tomislav Vlasic's attempt to form a prayer group,
has it begun well?

"Yes, it is good. Have him continue."

What should be done so that the authorities will not send away the
priests of the parish who work with faith and love?

"Pray and fast for this intention. I will tell you when the
moment comes what you must do."

Should Father Tomislav ask the parish to fast and pray in hopes that the Church will recognize the supernatural events taking place in Medjugorje?

"Yes, it is a good way. Have the parish pray for this gift. Have them pray also for the gift of the Holy Spirit so that all those who come here will feel the presence of God."

June 12, 1983

Concerning whether the priests should start new work around the church or ask permission from the authorities:

"Do not begin the work until receiving permission from the authorities. Otherwise, someone will inform the latter and the works would be forbidden. Go, and kindly request the authorization. It will be given to you."

June 14, 1983

Concerning what the priests should preach during the novena before the anniversary of the first apparitions:

"Have them do what they think is best. It would be good to remind the faithful of the events which have been happening here in relation to my coming. Have them remind the faithful of the reasons for my coming here."

Spring, 1983

"Hasten your conversion. Do not await the sign which has been announced for those who do not believe; it will be too late. You who believe, be converted and deepen your faith."

June 24, 1983

**"The sign will come, you must not worry about it. The only
thing that I would want to tell you is to be converted. Make
that known to all my children as quickly as possible. No pain,
no suffering is too great for me in order to save you. I will
pray to my Son not to punish the world; but I plead with you,
be converted.**

**"You cannot imagine what is going to happen nor what the
Eternal Father will send to earth. That is why you must be
converted! Renounce everything. Do penance. Express my
thanks to all my children who have prayed and fasted. I carry
all this to my Divine Son in order to obtain an alleviation of
His justice against the sins of mankind.**

**"I thank the people who have prayed and fasted. Persevere
and help me to convert the world."**

June 26, 1983

"Love your enemies. Pray for them and bless them."

July 1, 1983

This apparition took place at 11:00 p.m. on Cross Mountain.

**"I thank all those who have responded to my call. I bless all
of you. I bless each of you. In these days, I ask you to pray
for my intentions."**

Beginning of July, 1983

Regarding the problem with Bishop Zanic and the parish and
apparitions:

"Fast two days a week for the intentions of the Bishop, who
bears a heavy responsibility. If there is a need to, I will ask
for a third day. Pray each day for the Bishop."

July 26, 1983 - To Marija:

"Dear children, today I would like to invite you to constant
prayer and penance. Particularly, have the young people of
this parish become more active in their prayer."

August 6, 1983

Jakov questions Our Lady concerning orders from the Bishop to have
Father Pervan, the parish priest, stop the visionaries from saying the
Rosary and The Lord's Prayer, the Hail Mary, and the Glory Be the
customary seven times at the beginning of prayer:

"If it is so, then do not go against it so as not to provoke any
quarrels. If it is possible, talk about it tomorrow among
yourselves. All of you come to an agreement beforehand."

August 12, 1983

This apparition lasted longer than usual, approximately 38 minutes.

"Pray more for your spiritual life. Do your utmost in this
sense. Pray for your Bishop."

August 23, 1983

Concerning Canadian Fr. Tardiff, who has an important healing
ministry, Canadian Fr. Pierre Rancourt, and Dr. Madre, Deacon in
the Lion of Juda Community:

"I myself invited here each one of you, for I need you to spread
my messages in the entire world."

August 25, 1983

Concerning the arrest and expulsion of Father Tardif, Father
Raucourt, and Dr. Phillippe Madre by the Yugoslavian authorities:

"Do not worry for them. Everything is in God's plan."

August 29, 1983

Concerning a group of young people before they leave for their
pilgrimage to Siroki Brijeg at a youth festival:

**"I wish that you pray throughout your trip, and that you
glorify God. There, you will be able to meet other young
people. Convey the messages which I have given you. Do not
hesitate to speak to them about it. Some begin to pray and to
fast just as they have been told, but they get tired very quickly,
and thus loose the graces which they have acquired."**

September 5, 1983

Concerning Jakov's mother who died:

"Your mother is with me in Heaven."

September 12, 1983

**"Pray. When I give you this message, do not be content to just
listen to it. Increase your prayer and see how it makes you
happy. All graces are at your disposal. All you have to do is
to gain them. In order to do that, I tell you - Pray!"**

September 26, 1983

To Jakov:

"My Son suffers very much because the world is not
converting. May the world be converted and make peace."

October 15, 1983

"My Son suffers very much because men do not want to be
reconciled. They have not listened to me. Be converted, be
reconciled."

It is not certain whether this message and the September 26, 1983
message may have been duplicated by accident, or may have been
given twice.

October 21, 1983

"The important thing is to pray to the Holy Spirit so that He
may descend on you. When one has Him, one has everything.
People make a mistake when they turn only to the saints to
request something."

Advent, 1983

"Begin by calling on the Holy Spirit each day. The most
important thing is to pray to the Holy Spirit. When the Holy
Spirit descends on earth, then everything becomes clear and
everything is transformed."

November 26, 1983

In answer to a question, Our Lady said:

"Prayer and fasting."

November 30, 1983

To Marija, given for a priest:

"You must warn the Bishop very soon, and the Pope, with respect to the urgent and the great importance of the message for all mankind. I have already said many times that the peace of the world is in a state of crisis. Become brothers among yourselves; increase prayer and fasting in order to be saved."

December 26, 1983

To Ivan regarding a question asked by Father Laurentin:

"Our Lady prays for that. May he who undertakes it, do it in prayer. It is there that he will find his inspiration."

1983

"I know that many will not believe you, and that many who have an impassioned faith will cool off. You remain firm, and motivate people to instant prayer, penance and conversion. At the end, you will be happier."

To the Visionaries:

"When you will suffer difficulties, and need something, come to me."

Regarding cures:

"I cannot cure. God alone cures. Pray! I will pray with you. Believe firmly. Fast, do penance. I will help you as long as it is in my power to do it. God comes to help everyone. I am not God. I need your sacrifices and your prayers to help me."

Regarding Faith:

"Faith cannot be alive without prayer."

Regarding the Mass:

> "The Mass is the greatest prayer of God. You will never be able to understand its greatness. That is why you must be perfect and humble at Mass, and you should prepare yourselves there."

To a Priest who asks if it is preferable to pray to Our Lady or to Jesus:

> "I beseech you, pray to Jesus! I am His Mother, and I intercede for you with Him. But all prayers go to Jesus. I will help, I will pray, but everything does not depend solely on me, but also on your strength, and the strength of those who pray."

Regarding souls in Purgatory:

> "These persons wait for your prayers and your sacrifices."

On other topics:

> "The most beautiful prayer is the Creed."

> "The most important thing is to believe."

> "All prayers are good, if they are said with faith."

> "My Son wants to win all souls to Him, but the Devil strives to obtain something. The Devil makes a great effort to infiltrate among you, at all costs."

January, 1984

Advice to the pilgrims from Our Lady:

> "When you are in the room of the apparitions or at the church, you should not preoccupy yourselves with taking

pictures. **Rather, you should use the time to pray to Jesus, especially in those moments of particular grace during the apparitions."**

Lent, 1984

> **"Do not be afraid for yourselves, you are already saved. Pray rather for those who are in sin and who do not believe."**

ON MARCH 1, 1984, OUR LADY STARTED GIVING WEEKLY MESSAGES TO MARIJA PAVLOVIC FOR THE PARISH AND FOR THE WORLD. SEE CHAPTER 2 FOR THESE MESSAGES.

March 1, 1984

> **"Thursday (day of the Eucharist), may each one find his way to fast; he who smokes, may abstain from smoking; he who drinks alcohol, have him not drink. Have each one give up something which is dear to him. May these recommendations be conveyed to the parish."**

March 14, 1984

> **"Pray and fast so that the kingdom of God may come among you. Let my Son set you aglow with His fire."**

March 19, 1984

> **"Dear children, sympathize with me! Pray, pray, pray!"**

March 25, 1984 (ANNUNCIATION)

> **"Rejoice with me and with my angels because a part of my plan has already been realized. Many have been converted, but many do not want to be converted. Pray."**

This was the 1,000th apparition at Medjugorje, and after these above words, the Blessed Virgin sadly looked at the visionaries and cried.

March 28, 1984

"Many persons come here out of curiosity and not as pilgrims."

March 30, 1984

"I wish that your hearts would be united to mine, like my heart is united to that of my Son."

April 5, 1984

"If you would be strong in the faith, Satan would not be able to do anything against you. Begin to walk the path of my messages. Be converted, be converted, be converted."

April 8, 1984

"I ask you to pray for the conversion of everyone. For that, I need your prayers."

April 22, 1984 (EASTER SUNDAY)

"We all rejoice in Heaven. Rejoice with us!"

April 23, 1984

To the priests of Medjugorje:

"There is no need to give more information to the people, they already know what they are supposed to do."

April 24, 1984

Our Lady appeared very sad. With tears She said:

> "So many people, after they have begun to pray, to be converted, to fast, and to do penance here, quickly forget when they return to their homes and to their bad habits.

To the priests of Medjugorje:

> "The information suffices. People already know enough. Tell them this place is a place of prayer. Pray as much as you can, pray however you can, but pray more always. Each of you could pray even four hours a day. But I know that many do not understand because they think only of living for their work."

Father Vlasic questions Our Lady concerning telling the people to pray four hours a day and having them turn away. Our Lady then said:

> "Even you do not understand. It is hardly a sixth of your day."

June 13, 1984

> "Dear children, I invite you to pray more, you and the entire parish, until the day of the anniversary. Let your prayer become a sign of offering to God. Dear children, I know that you are all tired. You do not know how to offer yourselves to me. Offer yourselves completely to me these days."

June 24, 1984 (THIRD ANNIVERSARY)

> "My children, I thank you for each sacrifice that you have made during these days. Be converted, forgive each other, fast, pray, pray, pray!"

June 25, 1984

"Thank you for all your sacrifices."

June 26, 1984

"When I say, 'pray, pray, pray,' I do not only want to say to
increase the number of hours of prayer, but also to reinforce
the desire for prayer, and to be in contact with God. Place
yourself permanently in a state of spirit bathed in prayer."

July 16, 1984

"I pray for the priests and the parishioners, that no one may
be troubled. I know the changes which will take place soon [in
the parish clergy]. At the time of the changes, I will be there.
Also, do not be afraid; there will be in the future signs
concerning sinners, unbelievers, alcoholics, and young people.
They will accept me again."

July 20, 1984

Our Lady appears on Apparition Mountain in the late evening.

"Open your hearts to me, come close. Say in a loud voice your
intentions and your prayers."

Our Lady was very attentive to the prayers of the visionaries. While
praying for Bishop Zanic of Mostar, Her eyes filled up with tears
and She says:

"You are my little flowers. Continue to pray; my task is lighter
because of it."

She then blessed the visionaries and the people with a crucifix and
ascended back to heaven crying.

August 5, 1984 (OUR LADY'S TWO THOUSANDTH BIRTHDAY)

For three days before the celebration of the second millennium of Mary's birthday, there was fasting and continuous prayer. Confessions were heard by seventy priests without respite; great numbers of people were converted.

"Never in my life have I cried with sorrow, as I have cried this evening with joy. Thank you!"

In anticipation of this day, Our Lady said:

"The priests who will hear confessions will have great joy on that day."

The visionaries say Our Lady was "very joyful" during these three days of fasting and continuous prayer and Our Lady repeated:

"I am very happy! Continue, continue. Continue to pray and to fast. Continue and make me happy each day."

Later, the priests involved related that never in their lives had they felt such joy in their hearts.

August 6, 1984

"Continue and make me happy each day."

August 11, 1984 (SATURDAY)

"Dear children, pray, because Satan wishes to complicate my plans still further. Pray with the heart and surrender yourselves to Jesus in prayer."

August 25, 1984

To Mirjana:

"Wait for me September 13th; I will speak to you about the
future."

August 31, 1984

"I love the cross which you have providentially erected on
Mount Krizevac in a very special way. Go there more often
and pray."

October 8, 1984

Because Jakov was sick, Our Lady appeared to him at his home.

"Dear children, all the prayers which you recite in the evening
in your homes, dedicate them to the conversion of sinners
because the world is immersed in a great moral decay. Recite
the rosary each evening."

October 13, 1984

Concerning the Marian Movement of Priests:

"A message to you and to all those who love me: Dear
children, pray unceasingly and ask the Holy Spirit to inspire
you always. In everything that you ask, in everything that you
do, look only for the will of God. Live according to your
convictions and respect others."

October 20, 1984

"When you pray you must feel more. Prayer is a conversation
with God. To pray means to listen to God. Prayer is useful
for you because after prayer everything is clear. Prayer makes

one know happiness. Prayer can teach you how to cry. Prayer
can teach you how to blossom. Prayer is not a joke. Prayer
is a dialogue with God."

October 24, 1984

This apparition took place at 10:00 p.m. on Cross Mountain.

"My dear children, I am so happy to see you pray. Pray with
me so that God's plan may be realized thanks to your prayers
and to mine. Pray more, and more intensely."

October, 1984

"I would like to guide you spiritually, but I would not know
how to help you if you are not open. It suffices for you to
think, for example, where you were with your thoughts
yesterday during Mass. When you go to Mass, your trip from
home to church should be a time of preparation for Mass.
You should also receive Holy Communion with an open and
pure heart, with purity of heart, and with openness. Do not
leave the church without an appropriate act of thanksgiving.
I can help you only if you are accessible to my suggestions; I
can not help you if you are not open. The most important
thing in the spiritual life is to ask for the gift of the Holy
Spirit. When the Holy Spirit comes, then peace will be
established. When that occurs, everything changes around
you. Things will change."

October, 1984

While living in the Holy Land, Father Philip Pavich, O.F.M.,
requested Our Lady's pleasure about his moving to Medjugorje to
help English-speaking pilgrims. Through Ivan, Our Lady gave this
response:

"If he has the will, let him come to help us to spread God's message."

Father Philip arrived in May, 1987, to begin ministry in Medjugorje.

December 17, 1984

Concerning Monsignor Franic, Archbishop of Split.

"You will have to suffer more."

December 25, 1984

Although Our Lady did not give a message, She appeared carrying the Christ Child in Her arms.

1984

In response to a question about Oriental meditations such as Zen and Transcendental:

"Why do you call them 'meditations,' when it deals with human works? The true meditation is a meeting with Jesus. When you discover joy, interior peace, you must know there is only one God, and only one Mediator, Jesus Christ."* [See endnote, page 330.]

Regarding prayer:

"Your days will not be the same according to whether you pray, or you do not pray."* [See endnote, page 330.]

1984-1985

Mirjana reports:

"Tell the faithful that I need their prayers, and prayers from all the people. It is necessary to pray as much as possible and do penance because very few people have been converted up until now. There are many Christians who live like pagans. There are always so few true believers."

A Priest asked what they should do.

"Carry out your responsibility, and do what the Church asks you to do."

Jakov received a reproach from Our Lady because of his behavior toward his friends at school.

"You must love them all."

He responded that he did but that they are so annoying to him. Our Lady said:

"Then accept it as a sacrifice, and offer it."

Marija shares Our Lady's message with a group of seminarians from Zagreb and Djakovo who attended an apparition:

"Tell them, that with prayer, one obtains everything."

Mirjana asks Our Lady why She received a young nun with open arms but kept Her hands joined before the others.

"I will take with me very soon, all those to whom I extended my arms."

To a nun regarding her brother who had died in an accident:

"I understand the question. He died in the state of grace. He needs Masses and prayers."

Mirjana reported this message to a close friend, a religious:

"The hour has come when the demon is authorized to act with all his force and power. The present hour, is the hour of Satan."

"Many pretend to see Jesus and me, and to understand our words, but they are, in fact, lying. It is a very grave sin, and it is necessary to pray very much for them."

"I am anxious for people to know what is happening in Medjugorje. Speak about it, so that all will be converted."

Our Lady is questioned regarding her insistence in saying, "It presses me to ... ," by Mirjana:

"When you will be in Heaven, you will understand why I am so pressed."

To the Visionaries regarding the apparitions and their purpose:

"Is it, after all, that I bore you? Everything passes exactly according to God's plan. Have patience, persevere in prayer and in penance. Everything happens in its own time."

Responding to the confusion of a Catholic Priest over the cure of an Orthodox child:

"Tell this priest, tell everyone, that it is you who are divided on earth. The Muslims and the Orthodox, for the same reason as Catholics, are equal before my Son and me. You are all my children. Certainly, all religions are not equal, but all men are equal before God, as St. Paul says. It does not suffice to belong to the Catholic Church to be saved, but it is necessary to respect the commandments of God in following one's conscience.

"Those who are not Catholics, are no less creatures made in the image of God, and destined to rejoin someday, the House of the Father. Salvation is available to everyone, without exception. Only those who refuse God deliberately are condemned. To him who has been given little, little will be asked for. To whomever has been given much (to Catholics), very much will be required. It is God alone, in His infinite justice, Who determines the degree of responsibility and pronounces judgment."

January 2, 1985

This apparition of Our Lady, surrounded by angels, took place at 11:30 p.m. on Cross Mountain.

"I am very happy to have been able to come here for three years, thanks to the prayers of believers. Continue to pray thusly. A part of my plan has been realized. God blesses in a special way all those who are here. You can return happily to your homes. You do not immediately understand the reasons. Offer your prayers of thanksgiving for next week."

January 9, 1985

"I thank the faithful for having come to church in very bad and cold weather."

January 14, 1985

To Vicka:

"My dear children, Satan is strong. He wishes with all his strength to destroy my plans. Pray only, and do not stop doing it. I will also pray to my Son so that all the plans that I have begun will be realized. Be patient and persevere in prayer. Do not permit Satan to take away your courage. He works very hard in the world. Be on your guard."

February 3, 1985

> "I wish for Father Slavko to stay here, to guide the life, and to assemble all the news so that when I leave, there will be a complete image of everything that has happened here. I am also praying now for Slavko and for all those who work in this parish."

February 17, 1985

> "Pray, dear children, so that God's plan may be accomplished, and all the works of Satan be changed in favor of the glory of God."

February 25, 1985

To Marija:

> "For next week I invite you to say these words: 'I love God in everything.' With love, one obtains everything. You can receive many things, even the most impossible. The Lord wishes all the parishes to surrender to Him, and I too, in Him, desire it. Each evening, make your examination of conscience, but only to give thanks in acknowledgment for everything that His love offers us at Medjugorje."

End of February, 1985 or Early March, 1985

Our Lady was asked what should be done about all the discussions and publications regarding Medjugorje and She responded:

> "See! Now I am there, in each family, in each home. I am everywhere because I love. Do the same. The world lives from love."* [See endnote, page 330.]

After singing a song three times, Our Lady said:

"Excuse me for making you repeat, but I wish you to sing with the heart. You must really do everything with the heart."* [See endnote, page 330.]

Regarding the beginning of prayer: (The following two messages may be two versions of the same message)

"One has to be already prepared. If there are some sins, one must pull them out, otherwise, one will not be able to enter into prayer. If one has concerns, he should submit them to God."* [See endnote, page 330.]

"You must not preoccupy yourselves during prayer. During prayer, you must not be preoccupied with your sins. Sins must remain behind."* [See endnote, page 330.]

February, 1985 - March, 1985

"Dear children! You have always prayed that I not abandon you. Now I ask of you, in turn, not to abandon me. Especially during these days, Satan wants to disperse you. For that, pray very much these days. Dear children, I came again to thank you. You have not yet understood what that means, to give joy to my heart. It is a very great thing. I ask you only to persevere in prayer. As long as you pray, I will have words for you. Good-bye, I thank you dear children. My love for you is unlimited; be happy with me, because I am happy with you."

March 9, 1985

"You can receive a grace immediately, or in a month, or in ten years. I do not need The Lord's Prayer said a hundred or two hundred times. It is better to pray only one, but with a desire to encounter God. You should do everything out of love. Accept all annoyances, all difficulties, everything, with love. Dedicate yourselves to love."

March 13, 1985

This message was given to Vicka as a warning that she not make the same mistake as Ivan. Ivan had been persuaded to write down information concerning the sign and seal it in an envelop which was not to have been opened; however, it was and caused a stir.

"Pray, pray, pray! It is only with prayer that you will be able to avoid Ivan's error. He should not have written; and after that, he had to clearly acknowledge it so as not to plant any doubts."

March 18, 1985

To Mirjana:

"The Rosary is not an ornament for the home, as one often times limits himself to using it. Tell everyone to pray it.

"Right now many are greatly seeking money, not only in the parish, but in the whole world. Woe to those who seek to take everything from those who come, and blessed are those from whom they take everything.

"May the priests help you because I have entrusted to you a heavy burden, and I suffer from your difficulties. Ivan did not make a big mistake. I have sufficiently reprimanded him for the error. It is not necessary to scold him anymore."

March 24, 1985

"Today I wish to call you all to confession, even if you have confessed a few days ago. I wish that you all experience my feast day within yourselves. But you cannot experience it unless you abandon yourselves completely to God. Therefore, I am inviting you all to reconciliation with God!"

March 25, 1985 (THE ANNUNCIATION)

"Through my joy and the joy of this people, I say to all of you this evening, 'I love you and I wish you well.'"

April 5, 1985 (Good Friday)

To Ivanka:

"You, the members of this parish, have a large and heavy cross to bear; but do not be afraid to carry it. My Son is here to help you."

April 11, 1985 - September, 1987

The Closing of the Chapel

In a letter dated March 25, Bishop Zanic ordered that the Church and all contiguous rooms were forbidden to be used for the apparitions. They now begin taking place in a bedroom in the rectory.

April 15, 1985

"You must begin to work in your hearts as you work in the field. Work and change your hearts so that the new spirit of God can dwell there."

May 7, 1985

For at least an hour, Our Lady and two angels appeared to Ivanka at her home. More beautiful than ever, She asked Ivanka what she wished and approved of her request to see her mother. The mother of Ivanka soon appeared. Smiling, she embraced Ivanka, told her how proud she was of her, and embraced her again before she disappeared. During this apparition Our Lady said:

"My dear child, today is our last meeting, do not be sad. I will return to see you at each anniversary of the first apparition [June 25], beginning next year. Dear child, do not think that you have done anything bad, and that this would be the reason why I'm not returning near to you. No, it is not that. With all your heart you have accepted the plans which my Son and I formulated, and you have accomplished everything. No one in the world has had the grace which you, your brothers, and sisters have received. Be happy because I am your Mother and I love you from the bottom of my heart. Ivanka, thank you for the response to the call of my Son. Thank you for persevering and remaining always with Him as long as He will ask you. Dear child, tell all your friends that my Son and I are always with them when they call on us. What I have told you during these years on the secrets, do not speak to anyone about them. Go in the peace of God."

June 25, 1985 (FOURTH ANNIVERSARY OF THE FIRST APPARITION)

Marija asks Our Lady what She wants from the priests.

"I urge you to ask everyone to pray the Rosary. With the Rosary you will overcome all the troubles which Satan is trying to inflict on the Catholic Church. Let all priests pray the Rosary. Give time to the Rosary."

July 1, 1985

Our Lady appeared on Apparition Mountain

"I thank all those who have responded to my call. I bless all of you, I bless each of you. These days, I ask you to pray for my intentions. Go in the peace of God."

August 5, 1985   (BIRTHDAY OF OUR LADY - SPECIAL BLESSING)

The Church celebrates September 8 as Our Lady's birthday but She told the visionaries that August 5 is the actual date. Our Lady appeared dressed in golden splendor and was indescribable. She gives a special gift on Her birthday. This is the first time that She gives the SPECIAL BLESSING and She gives it several times later, generally on Feast Days. However, this blessing was not completely understood until August 15, 1988 when Marija spoke of it to a Caritas group in Medjugorje. (For an explanation of "THE SPECIAL BLESSING," see the November 29, 1988 message on Pages 256-258 in the American Message Section.

Our Lady said to Ivan:

> "Praised be Jesus Christ. My children, I'm happy to be with you this evening and to see you so numerous. I bless you with a Special Blessing. Make progress in holiness through the messages, I will help you. Give your utmost and we will go together, sensitive to the sweetness of life, light, and joy. Go in the peace of God, my children, my little children."

August 14, 1985

To Ivan:

> "Observe the complete fasts, Wednesdays and Fridays. Pray at least an entire Rosary: Joyous, Sorrowful and Glorious Mysteries."

August 15, 1985

To Mirjana:

> "My angel, pray for unbelievers. People will tear their hair, brothers will plead with brothers, they will curse their past

lives lived without God. They will repent, but it will be too
late. Now is the time for conversion. I have been exhorting
you for the past four years. Pray for them. Invite everyone to
pray the Rosary."

September 10, 1985

Regarding temptations from the devil:

"With respect to sin, it suffices to give it serious consideration,
and soon, move ahead and correct the sin."* [Endnote, Pg.330.]

"Your humility must be proud [high minded]. Your pride
should be humble."* [Jelena - See endnote, Page 330.]

"If you have received a gift from God, you must be proud but
do not say that it is yours. Say, rather, that it is God's."*
[See endnote, page 330.]

September, 1985

To Marija:

"I have given you my love, so that you may give it to others."

October 8, 1985

"Those who say, 'I do not believe in God,' how difficult it will
be for them when they will approach the Throne of God and
hear the voice: 'Enter into Hell.'"* [See endnote, page 330.]

October 21, 1985

A few weeks before Father Slavko's first visit to Medjugorje, he asked
the visionaries to ask Our Lady for a message for Ireland. When
Our Lady was first asked, She just smiled. Father Slavko again

asked the question a couple days before his trip and Our Lady
responded through Ivan:

> "That they may be the messengers of my messages: prayer,
> conversion, peace, and repentance, and that they may never
> forget that their mother loves them and prays for them."

October 25, 1985

To Mirjana concerning unbelievers:

> "They are my children. I suffer because of them. They do not
> know what awaits them. You must pray more for them."

Our Lady showed Mirjana the first secret - the earth was desolate:

> "It is the upheaval of a region of the world. In the world there
> are so many sins. What can I do, if you do not help me.
> Remember that I love you. God does not have a hard heart.
> Look around you and see what men do, then you will no longer
> say that God has a hard heart. How many people come to
> church, to the house of God, with respect, a strong faith, and
> love God? Very few! Here you have a time of grace and
> conversion. It is necessary to use it well."

Mirjana chose Father Petar Ljubicic to reveal the secrets to the
world. Ten days before the first secret is to be revealed, Father Petar
will be given a parchment containing the ten secrets. This parchment
was given to Mirjana by Our Lady. Anyone can see this parchment
but it cannot be read by those viewing it. When Father Petar
receives the parchment, he will only be able to read the first secret.
During the ten days, Father Petar is to spend the first seven days in
fasting and prayer. Three days before the event takes place, he is to
announce it to the world. At the proper time, he will be able to see
and read the second secret, and then the third, etc., according to the
schedule of Heaven.

"Pray very much for Father Petar, to whom I send a Special
Blessing. I am a mother, that is why I come. You must not
fear for I am here."

November 16, 1985

After an hour of prayers of petition, Our Lady says:

"Have you forgotten that you are in my hands?"* [See
endnote, page 330.]

December 4, 1985

Marija questions Our Lady regarding discernment sought by Gianni
Sgreva, an Italian Passionist who was inspired to found a "Community
of Consecrated," on the message of Medjugorje:

"I prefer to answer him personally."

This community opened on May 18, 1987. (See message on June 7,
1986.)

1985

"Let the faithful meditate each day on the life of Jesus, while
praying the rosary."

"Every prayer, which comes from the heart, is agreeable to
God."

"You do not celebrate the Eucharist, as you should. If you
would know what grace, and what gifts you receive, you would
prepare yourselves for it each day, for an hour at least. You
should go to confession once a month. You should consecrate
three days to reconciliation, each month: the first Friday of
the month, followed by Saturday, and Sunday."

In Medjugorje the following has been established: an hour of
adoration before the Most Blessed Sacrament on each Thursday; an
hour of devotion before the crucifix with prayers for sinners on each
Friday; and two late evening (10:30 p.m.) Adoration Services on
Wednesday and Saturday nights.

Undated

A sculptor was asked to do a statue of the Blessed Mother and he
said, "Only if Our Lady wants it."   When the visionaries asked Our
Lady about this, She said:

**"Do one of Jesus instead, but be inspired by the words, 'COME
TO ME ALL WHO ARE WEARY.'"**

January 6, 1986

To Vicka:

**"If you agree to it, I will not appear to you anymore for 50
days."**

Vicka agreed to this.

March 18, 1986

Father Milan Mikulich called Mirjana Dragicevic and asked her to
pray for Danica Radic who was suffering from liver disease for seven
years.   During Mirjana's birthday apparition Our Lady said:

"Danica will be alright.   She will need human help."

In October, 1988, Danica received a successful liver transplant and as
of March, 1990, she is doing extremely well and is working.

March 24, 1986

To the Prayer Group:

"Dear children, receive all that the Lord offers you. Do not
have your hands paralyzed and do not repeat, 'Jesus, give
me.' But open your hands, and take everything that the Lord
offers you."

March 25, 1986 (ANNUNCIATION)

"Today, before God, I say my 'Fiat' for all of you. I repeat it:
I say my 'Fiat' for all of you.
Dear children, pray, so that in the whole world may come the
Kingdom of Love. How mankind would be happy if love
reigned!"* [See endnote, page 330.]

April 17, 1986

To the prayer group which questioned Our Lady's advice regarding
watching television and reading newspapers as too difficult:

"If you look at the programs, if you look at the newspapers,
your heads are filled with news, then there is no longer any
place for me in your hearts.

"Pray. Fast. Let God act!

"Pray for the gift of love, for the gift of faith, for the gift of
prayer, for the gift of fasting."* [See endnote, page 330.]

The Week Preceding May 3, 1986

To the prayer group:

"I give you the best that I can give anyone. I give myself and
my Son."* [See endnote, page 330.]

May 3, 1986

For Marija's prayer group:

> **"Dear children, seek to make your hearts happy through the means of prayer. Dear children, be the joy for all mankind, be the hope of mankind. You will only be able to obtain it through the means of prayer. Pray, pray!"*** [See endnote, page 330.]

Toward May 12, 1986

To the prayer group:

> **"You will be happy if you do not judge yourselves according to your faults, but if you understand that in your faults even graces are offered to you."*** [See endnote, page 330.]

June 6, 1986

> **"Love. If you do not love, you are not able to transmit the testimony. You are not able to witness, either for me, or for Jesus."*** [See endnote, page 330.]

June 7, 1986

Through Marija concerning Father Pere Gianni Sgreva, who wanted to organize a new community based on the messages of Medjugorje:

> **"Yes, one must pray. What you are doing pleases me. For the time being, keep a very active prayer life, and God will then light up the other plans."**

June 20, 1986

> **"Pray before the Crucifix. Special graces come from the Crucifix. Consecrate yourselves to the Cross. Do not**

blaspheme either Jesus or the Crucifix."* [See endnote, page 330.]

June 24, 1986 (SPECIAL BLESSING)

There were 30,000 to 50,000 people present. This is the third time Our Lady gives the SPECIAL BLESSING in which those receiving it may bless others in Our Lady's name.

To Marija and Ivan with the Prayer Group on Cross Mountain:

> "You are on a Tabor. You receive blessings, strength, and love. Carry them into your families and into your homes. To each one of you, I grant a Special Blessing. Continue in joy, prayer, and reconciliation."

To the Prayer Group:

> "I beseech you, withdraw in silence. Your obligation is not so much to do, but to adore God, to stay with Him."

June 26, 1986

> "You will have as many graces as you want. That depends on you. You will have love when you want it, as long as you want it. That depends on you."* [See endnote, page 330.]

July 10, 1986

To the prayer group after an evaluation:

> "I thank you for that. You have done well, but do not forget (. . .); basically, God's will is decisive."* [See endnote, page 330.]

August 4, 1986

> **"I wish only that for you the Rosary become your life."*** [See endnote, page 330.]

August 5, 1986

> **"Read each Thursday the Gospel of Matthew, where it is said: 'No one can serve two masters . . . . You cannot serve God and money.'"*** [See endnote, page 330.]

September 12, 1986

> **"Many have begun to pray for healing here at Medjugorje, but, when they have returned to their homes, they abandon prayer, forget, and also lose many graces."*** [See endnote, page 330.]

October 6, 1986

Permission was given by Fr. Pervan for an individual from Birmingham, Alabama, to ask Marija to present a question to Our Lady. The individual explained why he would like this asked of Our Lady as well as other information concerning the Birmingham area so that Marija would have a clear understanding of why this was desired. After discussing several things about the region, Marija requested to keep the question and stated that if Our Lady gave an answer, (many times She gives no answer), she would write it down and return it following the apparition that night.

The question: "Dear Blessed Mother, if it is God's will, we humbly ask that the conversion taking place in Medjugorje be allowed to take place in the Parish of Blessed Sacrament in Alabama and that it 'divinely' be spread throughout the whole region. We surrender this Parish to you and ask if there is anything you request." Marija and Jakov went to the kitchen and Marija wrote down Our Lady's answer which starts off with, "Gospa says": (Gospa means Blessed Mother.)

"Pray and by your life witness. Not with words but rather through prayer will you attain what your desire is. Therefore, pray more and live in humility."

Below is a photo of Our Lady's above response, written in Marija's handwriting in Croatian.

Our Lady's answer was prophetic and not completely understood until November 18, 1988 when Marija came to Birmingham, Alabama, and Our Lady prayed, blessed, and converted tens of thousands of people who travelled there from as far away as South America, the Caribbean, and even Russia. (See American Messages, Page 253.)

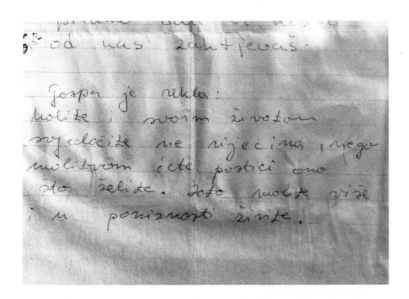

Above is Our Lady's answer in Marija's handwriting.

December 29, 1986

An answer for Father Tomislav Vlasic about his writing to address lies and injustices:

"Do not waste your time. Pray and love. You cannot even imagine how powerful God is."* [See endnote, page 330.]

1986

The following is an answer from Our Lady regarding Church authority and the Church's approval of the apparitions in Medjugorje.

"One must follow the authority of the Church with certainty. Yet, before she expresses an opinion, it is necessary to advance spiritually, because she will not be able to express a judgment in a vacuum, but in a confirmation which presupposes growth of the child. First comes birth, followed by Baptism, then Confirmation. The Church comes to confirm him, who is born of God. We must walk and advance in the spiritual life, affected by these messages."

Undated

To Vicka:

"Do you want to offer yourself, also, for the salvation of the world? I need your sacrifices."* [See endnote, page 330.]

January 28, 1987

To Mirjana, at Sarajevo:

"My dear children! I come to you in order to lead you to purity of soul and then to God. How have you listened to me? At the beginning without believing and with fear and defiance toward these young people whom I have chosen, then afterwards, most of you listened to me in your heart and began to carry out my maternal requests. But that did not last for long. Whenever I come to you my Son comes with me, but so does Satan. You permitted, without noticing, his influences on you and he drives you on. Sometimes you understand that something you have done is not agreeable to God, but quickly you no longer pay attention to it.

"Do not let that happen, my children. Wipe from my face the tears that I cry in seeing what you do. Wake up to yourselves. Take time to meet with God in the church. Come to visit in your Father's house. Take the time to meet among yourselves for family prayer and implore the grace of God. Remember your deceased. Give them joy with the celebration of the Holy Mass. Do not look with scorn on those who beg you for a piece of bread. Do not turn them away from your full tables. Help them and God will also help you. Perhaps it is in this way that God will hear you, and the blessing that He wants to give you in thanks will be realized.

"You have forgotten all this my children. Satan has influenced you also in this. Do not let that happen! Pray with me! Do not deceive yourselves into thinking, "I am good, but my brother next door is no good." You would be wrong. I, your Mother, love you and it is for that reason that I am warning you about this. Concerning the secrets, my children, these are not known by the people. But when they will learn of them, it will be too late. Return to prayer! There is nothing more important! I would dearly wish that the Lord would permit me to enlighten you a little more on these secrets, but the grace which is offered to you is already great enough.

"Think how much you have offended Him. What are you offering to Him of yourself? When was the last time you renounced something for the Lord? I no longer wish to reprimand you in this way, but I want to invite you once more to prayer, fasting, and penance. If you wish to obtain a grace from God by fasting, then let no one know that you are fasting. If you wish to receive a grace from God by a gift to the poor, let no one know except you and the Lord that you have given this gift. Listen to me, my children! Meditate on my message in prayer."

March 21, 1987

To Vicka in Zagreb:

> "I bless you with the benediction of a Mother. Pray every day
> and confide yourselves to my son, Jesus. In this way you will
> understand what God asks of each of you."

March 22, 1987

Vicka related the apparition of March 22: "Right away She held Her
hands over us and said an interior prayer that I did not understand.
She came surrounded by five little angels. Then She confided a few
things to me and left."

June 24, 1987 (SPECIAL BLESSING)

On June 24, 1987, at 11:30 p.m., Our Lady asked everyone to come
to the mountain (of the Cross) for a special apparition. Close to
50,000 people were there while a military helicopter hovered
overhead. It flew away three or four minutes prior to the apparition
at 11:25 p.m. It came back, presumedly to refuel near Mostar, five
to ten minutes after the apparition ended. Several times the lights
from the helicopter flooded the crowd. The apparition lasted about
ten minutes. A recount from Marija of the apparition follows. . . .

Anniversary Apparition: Tonight when Our Lady came She was
happy and She immediately prayed over all of us for a certain amount
of time. We asked Her for a blessing. Then She spoke to us and
gave a message which sounds like this:

> "Dear children, I want to lead you to the path of conversion
> and I wish that you convert the world, that your life be
> conversion for others."

Then Our Lady said She does not want us to be unfaithful and She
desires each of us to surrender ourself fully to Her will and the will

of God. Our Lady said from today She is granting us special graces, and She's giving us, especially, a gift of conversion so that all of us can take the blessing with us to our homes and truly encourage others to conversion. God gave us the gift tonight through Our Lady. Then Our Lady prayed over all of us for some time. We prayed with Her for the needs of each one of us who were here tonight. Our Lady said, **"Go in God's Peace,"** and then She left.

1987

In response to being questioned whether She wanted to create a new order or a new structure or a particular "Medjugorje Community," Our Lady said:

"Children of mine, you don't know what you ask. You don't know what is waiting for you. You cannot comprehend the plans of God! I ask of you that you accomplish what I show you."

1987

"Love your Serbian Orthodox and Muslim brothers, and the atheists who persecute you."

"All your prayers touch me very much, especially your daily rosary."

March 18, 1988

Mirjana had an apparition on her birthday which lasted only four or five minutes. Our Lady asked her,

"Pray for unbelievers."

June 25, 1988

During Ivanka's anniversary apparition, she said to the crowd who
had gathered at her home, "Our Lady wishes for all present to kneel
down." After Our Lady ascended back to heaven, Ivanka went
outside and announced to the crowd that when Our Lady asked
everyone to kneel down, She gave them a SPECIAL BLESSING and
said,

"The people here will be witnesses of the love of God."

She then told the group that Our Lady spoke of the third and fourth
secrets.

Approximately the First Quarter of 1989

In a recent message to Vicka Ivankovic, when the visionary was
visiting Bologna, Italy, Our Lady again asked for prayers for young
people:

**"Dear children, I again ask you to pray for all the young
people of the world because they find themselves in a difficult
situation. You can help them with your love and prayers of
the heart."**

January 26, 1989

Jakov says, "Our Lady is very sad because of the sinners in this world.
She is also very sad because we don't live Her messages. Our Lady
asks for prayer especially in the families for these two intentions."

March 18, 1989

This is Mirjana's Birthday Apparition. Our Lady appeared sad, very
sad. This is rare. Our Lady then said:

"One more time I beseech all of you to pray, to help by your prayers the unbelievers, those who do not have the grace to experience God in their hearts with a living faith. I do not want to threaten again! My wish is just to warn you all as a Mother. I beg you for people who do not know about the secrets.... I want to tell you how I suffer for all because I am the Mother of all."

April, 1989

This date is approximate. In April Mirjana made this statement: "I'd like to relay to the young people a petition from Our Lady." The petition is:

"If they can't believe in God, they should spend at least five minutes a day in silent meditation. During that time, they should think about the God they say doesn't exist."

June 25, 1989

This is Ivanka's Annual Apparition which lasted approximately eight minutes in all. In 1988, Our Lady spoke to her about the third and fourth secrets and in 1989, as if continuing that discussion, She spoke about the fifth secret. After the apparition, Ivanka immediately wrote down an important message which Our Lady had given her. The following is the message:

"Pray because you are in great temptation and danger because the world and material goods lead you into slavery. Satan is active in this plan. I want to help each of you in prayer. I am interceding to my Son for you."

February 2, 1990

Mirjana received this apparition in Portland, Oregon in the United States of America while visiting Father Milan Mekulich who presided at her marriage. For over a year, Mirjana has been receiving

interior locutions on the second day of each month but on this
occasion she was graced by an apparition and a message for the
world.

> "I have been with you nine years. For nine years I wanted to
> tell you that God, your Father, is the only way, truth and life.
> I wish to show you the way to Eternal Life. I wish to be your
> tie, your connection to the profound faith. LISTEN TO ME!

> "Take your rosary and get your children, your families with
> you. This is the way to come to salvation. Give your good
> example to your children: give a good example to those who
> do not believe. You will not have happiness on this earth,
> neither will you come to Heaven if you are not with pure and
> humble hearts, and do not fulfill the law of God. I am asking
> for your help to join me to pray for those who do not believe.
> You are helping me very little. You have little charity or love
> for your neighbor and God gave you the love and showed you
> how you should forgive and love others. For that reason,
> reconcile and purify your soul. TAKE YOUR ROSARY AND
> PRAY IT. All your sufferings take patiently. You should
> remember that Jesus was patiently suffering for you.

> "Let me be your Mother and your tie to God, to the Eternal
> Life. Do not impose your faith on the unbelievers. Show it to
> them by your example and pray for them. MY CHILDREN,
> PRAY!"

Mirjana told Fr. Milan that Our Lady was referring to the Sacrament
of Reconciliation, for Catholics, when She said. "...reconcile and
purify your soul."

Undated

For several years the visionary, Vicka, had been suffering from an
inoperable brain cyst which caused her terrible headaches. During
the course of her illness, Our Lady continued to appear to her and

once, on her way to the hospital in Zagreb, Our Lady offered her two
choices, saying:

**"I will give you health with no apparitions or I will give you
your cross with apparitions."**

Because she had been suffering so tremendously she chose health but
later regretted it. After forty days of not having apparitions, Our
Lady appeared to her and gave her the offer once again. She joyfully
took her cross back. (Vicka was miraculously healed in 1988 and as
of this writing, remains so.)

June 25, 1990

Ivanka ceased seeing Our Lady on a regular basis after her May 7,
1985 apparition; however, Our Lady promised to visit her each June
25th [the anniversary of the beginning of the apparitions in
Medjugorje] for the rest of her life.

Ivanka had just given birth to her second child ten days before so no
one except close family was allowed to be present during the
apparition. The following is the account of the June 25, 1990
apparition.

With her family, Ivanka prayed the Rosary. Upon finishing it and
just prior to 6:40 p.m., Ivanka prayed The Lord's Prayer, the Hail
Mary, and the Glory Be three times each. Our Lady then appeared
to her and Ivanka saw Her in three dimensions, just as anyone would
see someone before them - except Our Lady was floating on a cloud
and was radiant. She came without angels and with Her hands
stretched out. Our Lady was very joyful and happy. She blessed all
who had recommended their prayers to Her.

In 1988 Our Lady spoke to Ivanka about the third and fourth secrets.
During that period of the apparition on June 25, 1988, Ivanka's face
became very serious and grave. That apparition lasted 15 minutes.
Ivanka's 1989 apparition lasted eight minutes. During some of that

time, as if continuing where She left off, Our Lady spoke to Ivanka about the first part of the fifth secret. Again this year, Our Lady continued, this time speaking about the last half of the fifth secret. During this time, Our Lady was not happy and it was reflected in Ivanka's face.

Remarkably during this apparition, Ivanka again saw her mother who had died a couple of months before the apparitions began in 1981. Ivanka said Her mother just smiled at her. Possibly because Ivanka had just given birth, Our Lady said:

"I thank you for giving your life to allow other life."

The apparition lasted approximately nine minutes. Our Lady ended by saying,

"Go with God, my dear children."

January 11, 1991

Marija was sick and Our Lady appeared to her in her room.

"I need your prayers and sacrifices for peace."

Ivan was with thirty priests who were on retreat in Medjugorje. During his 5:40 p.m. apparition, Our Lady was happy to see all the priests, blessed all of them, and asked the priests to pray for peace.

March 18, 1991

The following is Mirjana's description of her annual birthday apparition:

"Five days before my birthday, while in prayer, I found out that Our Lady would appear to me at 7:30 p.m. On that evening, many people gathered and we prayed. Exactly at 7:30 p.m. She appeared, this time not as sad as last year. You could say Her mood was normal. This time no light preceded Her as it did during the time of Her daily apparitions. She stayed for seven minutes. Upon leaving, the Heavens opened and I saw three angels waiting for Her. Only in August 1981 had I seen the angels waiting for Her like this after She had been with us.

"On this occasion She did not speak to me about the' secrets. During the apparition I prayed three "Our Fathers" with Her, one for non-believers, one for all those who needed it, and one for all the sick who were present. She then blessed all of us and all the holy objects that had been brought to Her.

"I also had a lot of questions to ask, given to me by others. For all those who asked something, She gave but one answer:

"**"Pray all three mysteries of the Rosary daily for non-believers and attend Mass specially for them once a month. God knows what their own needs are which they must bring to Him.""**

The following is the message from Our Lady given to Mirjana in Bijakovici during her annual apparition:

"Dear children! I am glad that you have gathered in such a large number. I would desire that you gather often in communal prayer to my Son.

"Most of all I would desire that you dedicate prayers for my children who do not know my love and the love of my Son. Help them to come to know it! Help me as a Mother of all of you!

"My children, how many times I have already invited you here in Medjugorje to prayer and I will invite you again because I desire you to open your hearts to my Son, to allow Him to come in and fill you with peace and love. Allow Him, let Him enter!

**"Help Him by your prayers in order that you might be able to
spread peace and love to others, because that is now most
necessary for you in this time of battle with Satan.**

**"I have often spoken to you: pray, pray, because only by means
of prayer will you drive off Satan and all the evil that goes
along with him.**

**"I promise you, my children, that I will pray for you, but I seek
from you more vigorous prayers and I seek you to spread
peace and love which I am asking you in Medjugorje already
nearly ten years.**

"Help me, and I will pray my Son for you."

Date Unknown

"You have forgotten the Bible."

This message was possibly given to Father Jozo. He has described
never seeing a mother so sad as the Mother of God when She talked
about the Bible.

The following message is not included in the indexes.

June 25, 1991 (IVANKA'S ANNUAL APPARITION)

Our Lady appeared to Ivanka for approximately eight minutes. Many
crowded in her living room. Ivanka's facial expressions ranged from
intensely serious to supremely joyful. Ivanka recommended all
present to Our Lady. She said Our Lady spoke to her about the first
half of the sixth secret.

It has been realized that during Ivanka's last four annual apparitions
Our Lady has spoken about the secrets in progression. In 1988, Our
Lady spoke about the third and fourth secrets. In 1989, She spoke
about the first half of the fifth secret. In 1990, as if continuing where

She left off the previous year, Our Lady spoke about the last half of the fifth secret. In 1991, Our Lady spoke to her about the first half of the sixth secret. Everything Our Lady does and says is done for a reason. The discussion of these secrets in this progression is in itself a message to us.

Ivanka stated that Our Lady said:

"I pray that you pray more strongly* for peace and that you become more rooted in faith."

*   The Croatian word which was used means 'unbreakable.' The closest gramatically-correct English translation is 'more strongly.' The English translation, 'more strongly,' is weaker than the word which Our Lady used meaning 'unbreakable.'

NOTES AND FUTURE EXPANSION
OF OUR LADY'S MESSAGES

CHAPTER 2

THE WEEKLY MESSAGES
OF OUR LADY
THROUGH MARIJA

(March 1, 1984 to January 8, 1987)

"PLEASE DO NOT LET MY HEART WEEP TEARS OF BLOOD."
(May 24, 1984)

These messages were given for the parish and to all in the world who
want to live them. The weekly and monthly messages for the Parish
are always given to Marija.

March 1, 1984

>"Dear children, I have chosen this parish in a special way and
>I wish to lead it. I am guarding it in love and I want everyone
>to be mine. Thank you for having responded tonight. I wish
>you always to be with my Son and me in ever greater numbers.
>I shall speak a special message to you every Thursday."

March 8, 1984

>"Thank you for having responded to my call. Dear children,
>you in the parish, be converted. This is my other wish. That
>way all those who shall come here shall be able to convert."

March 15, 1984

This day, like every Thursday evening, the faithful were worshipping
the Most Holy Sacrament, but this evening it was noticed that many
people remained in the church for adoration, although they had
worked hard in the fields.

> "Tonight also, dear children, I am grateful to you in a special
> way for being here. Unceasingly adore the Most Blessed
> Sacrament of the Altar. I am always present when the faithful
> are adoring. Special graces are then being received."

March 22, 1984

> "Dear children, in a special way this evening, I am calling you
> during Lent to honor the wounds of my Son, which He received
> from the sins of this parish. Unite yourselves with my prayers
> for the parish so that His sufferings may be bearable. Thank
> you for having responded to my call. Try to come in ever
> greater numbers."

March 29, 1984

> "Dear children, in a special way this evening, I am calling you
> to perseverance in trials. Consider how the Almighty is still
> suffering today on account of your sins. So when sufferings
> come, offer them up as a sacrifice to God. Thank you for
> having responded to my call."

April 5, 1984

> "Dear children, this evening I pray that you especially venerate
> the Heart of my Son, Jesus. Make reparation for the wound
> inflicted on the Heart of my Son. That Heart is offended by
> all kinds of sin. Thank you for coming this evening.

April 12, 1984

"Dear children, today I beseech you to stop slandering and to pray for the unity of the parish, because my Son and I have a special plan for this parish. Thank you for having responded to my call."

April 19, 1984 (HOLY THURSDAY)

"Dear children, sympathize with me! Pray, pray, pray!"

April 26, 1984

Although this was Thursday, Our Lady gave no messages; therefore, Marija concluded that perhaps Our Lady would give the Thursday messages only during Lent.

April 30, 1984 (MONDAY)

Today is Monday and Marija asked Our Lady, "Dear Madonna, why didn't you give me a message for the parish on Thursday?" Our Lady replied to Marija:

"I don't wish to force anyone to do that which he neither feels nor desires, even though I had special messages for the parish by which I wanted to awaken the faith of every believer. But only a really small number has accepted my Thursday messages. In the beginning there were quite a few. But it's become a routine affair for them. And now recently some are asking for the message out of curiosity, and not out of faith and devotion to my Son and me."

May 3, 1984

No message was given.

May 10, 1984

Many of the faithful felt shaken by the last message of Our Lady. Some had the feeling that Our Lady would not give any more messages to the parish, but this evening She said:

> **"I am speaking to you and I wish to speak further. You, just listen to my instructions!"**

May 17, 1984

> **"Dear children, today I am very happy because there are many who want to consecrate themselves to me. Thank you. You have not made a mistake. My Son, Jesus Christ, wishes to bestow on you special graces through me. My Son is happy because of your dedication. Thank you for having responded to my call."**

May 24, 1984

> **"Dear children, I have told you already that I have chosen you in a special way, just the way you are. I, the Mother, love you all. And in any moment that is difficult for you, do not be afraid! Because I love you even when you are far from my Son and me. Please, do not let my heart weep with tears of blood because of the souls who are being lost in sin. Therefore, dear children, pray, pray, pray! Thank you for having responded to my call."**

May 31, 1984 (ASCENSION THURSDAY)

There were many people present from abroad. Our Lady did not give a message for the parish. She told Marija that She would give a message on Saturday to be announced at the Sunday parish Mass.

June 2, 1984 (SATURDAY)

Today is Saturday, one of the days during which the Novena to the Holy Spirit (prior to Pentecost) is being conducted. The message to Marija is:

"Dear children, tonight I wish to tell you during the days of this novena to pray for the outpouring of the Holy Spirit on your families and on your parish. Pray, and you shall not regret it. God will give you gifts by which you will glorify Him till the end of your life on this earth. Thank you for having responded to my call."

June 7, 1984

No message was given today. Our Lady promised to give it on Saturday.

June 9, 1984 (SATURDAY)

Today is Saturday, the Vigil of Pentecost, and once again Our Lady did not give a Thursday message for the parish; however, She promised to give the message this evening. The message is:

"Dear children, tomorrow night pray for the Spirit of Truth! Especially, you from the parish. Because you need the Spirit of Truth to be able to convey the messages just the way they are, neither adding anything to them, nor taking anything whatsoever away from them, but just the way I said them. Pray for the Holy Spirit to inspire you with the spirit of prayer, so you will pray more. I, your Mother, tell you that you are praying little. Thank you for having responded to my call."

June 14, 1984

No special message was given.

June 21, 1984

"Pray, pray, pray!   Thank you for having responded to my call."

June 28, 1984

No special message was given.

July 5, 1984

"Dear children, today I wish to tell you, always pray before your work and end your work with prayer. If you do that, God will bless you and your work. These days you have been praying too little and working a lot; therefore, pray. In prayer, you will find rest. Thank you for your response to my call."

July 12, 1984

"Dear children, these days Satan wants to frustrate my plans. Pray that his plan not be realized. I will pray to my Son, Jesus, to give you the grace to experience the victory of Jesus in the temptations of Satan. Thank you for having responded to my call."

July 19, 1984

"Dear children, these days you have been experiencing how Satan is working. I am always with you, and do not be afraid of temptations because God is always watching over us. Also I have given myself to you and I sympathize with you even in the smallest temptation. Thank you for having responded to my call."

July 26, 1984

"Dear children, today also I would like to call you to persistent prayer and penance. Especially, let the young people of this

parish be more active in their prayers. **Thank you for having responded to my call.**"

August 9, 1984

"**Dear children, Satan continues to hinder my plans. Pray, pray, pray! In prayer, abandon yourselves to God. Pray with the heart. Thank you for your response to my call.**"

August 14, 1984 (TUESDAY)

This apparition was unexpected. Ivan was praying at home. After that he started to get ready to go to Church for the evening services. By surprise Our Lady appeared to him and told him to relate to the people.

"**I would like the people to pray along with me these days. Pray all the more. Pray as much as possible! Fast strictly on Wednesdays and Fridays, and every day pray at least one Rosary: the Joyful, Sorrowful, and Glorious Mysteries.**"

Our Lady asked that we accept this message with a firm will. She especially requested this of the parishioners and believers from the surrounding places.

August 16, 1984

"**Dear children, I beseech you, especially those from this parish, to live my messages and convey them to others, to whomever you meet. Thank you for having responded to my call.**"

August 23, 1984

"**Pray, pray, pray!**"

Marija said that She also invited the people, and especially the young people, to keep order during the Mass.

August 30, 1984

This message was regarding the cross, erected on Mount Krizevac in 1933 for the 1,950th anniversary of the Death and Resurrection of Jesus:

"Dear children, the cross was also in God's plan when you built it. These days especially, go on the mountain and pray before the cross. I need your prayers. Thank you for having responded to my call."

September 6, 1984

"Dear children, without prayer there is no peace. Therefore, I say to you, dear children, pray at the foot of the crucifix for peace. Thank you for having responded to my call."

September 13, 1984

"Dear children, I still need your prayers. You wonder why all these prayers? Look around you, dear children, and you will see how greatly sin has dominated the world. Pray, therefore, that Jesus conquers. Thank you for having responded to my call."

September 20, 1984

"Dear children, today I call on you to begin fasting with the heart. There are many people who are fasting, but only because everyone is fasting. It has become a custom which no one wants to stop. I ask the parish to fast out of gratitude because God has allowed me to stay this long in this parish. Dear children, fast and pray with the heart. Thank you for having responded to my call."

September 27, 1984

"Dear children, you have helped me along by your prayers to realize my plans. Keep on praying that my plans be completely realized. I request the families of the parish to pray the Family Rosary. Thank you for your response to my call."

October 4, 1984

"Dear children, today I want to tell you that again and again you make me happy by your prayer, but there are enough of those in this very parish who do not pray and my heart is saddened. Therefore, pray that I can bring all your sacrifices and prayers to the Lord. Thank you for having responded to my call."

October 11, 1984

In this message, Our Lady refers to a testing. This testing was a long rain during the middle of the reaping season which caused a great deal of damage to the crops.

"Dear children, thank you for dedicating all your hard work to God even now when He is testing you through the grapes you are picking. Be assured, dear children, that He loves you and, therefore, He tests you. You just always offer up all your burdens to God and do not be anxious. Thank you for having responded to my call."

October 18, 1984

"Dear children, today I call on you to read the Bible every day in your homes and let it be in a visible place so as always to encourage you to read it and to pray. Thank you for having responded to my call."

October 25, 1984

"Dear children, pray during this month. God allows me every
day to help you with graces to defend yourselves against evil.
This is my month. I want to give it to you. You just pray and
God will give you the graces you are seeking. I will help along
with it. Thank you for having responded to my call."

November 1, 1984

"Dear children, today I call you to the renewal of prayer in
your homes. The work in the fields is over. Now devote
yourselves to prayer. Let prayer take the first place in your
families. Thank you for having responded to my call."

November 8, 1984

"Dear children, you are not conscious of the messages which
God is sending to you through me. He is giving you great
graces and you do not comprehend them. Pray to the Holy
Spirit for enlightenment. If you only knew how great are the
graces God is granting you, you would be praying without
ceasing. Thank you for having responded to my call."

November 15, 1984

"Dear children, you are a chosen people and God has given you
great graces. You are not conscious of every message which I
am giving you. Now I just want to say--pray, pray, pray! I
don't know what else to tell you because I love you and I want
you to comprehend my love and God's love through prayer.
Thank you for having responded to my call."

November 22, 1984

"Dear children, these days live all the main messages
[conversion, confession, prayer, fasting and Holy Mass] and

keep rooting them into your hearts till Thursday. Thank you for having responded to my call."

November 29, 1984

"Dear children, no, you don't know how to love and you don't know how to listen with love to the words I am saying to you. Be conscious, my beloved, that I am your Mother and I have come on earth to teach you how to listen out of love, to pray out of love and not compelled by the fact that you are carrying a cross. By means of the cross, God is glorified through every person. Thank you for having responded to my call."

December 6, 1984

"Dear children, these days I am calling you to family prayer. In God's Name, many times I have been giving you messages, but you have not listened to me. This Christmas will be unforgettable for you only if you accept the messages which I am giving you. Dear children, don't allow that day of joy to become my most sorrowful day. Thank you for having responded to my call."

December 13, 1984

"Dear children, you know that the season of joy is getting closer, but without love you will achieve nothing. So first of all, begin to love your own family, everyone in the parish, and then you'll be able to love and accept all who are coming over here. Now let these seven days be a week when you need to learn to love. Thank you for having responded to my call."

December 20, 1984

"Dear children, today I am asking you to do something concrete for Jesus Christ. As a sign of dedication to Jesus, I want each family of the parish to bring a single flower before that happy day. I want every member of the family to have a single flower by the crib so Jesus can come and see your dedication to Him! Thank you for having responded to my call."

December 27, 1984

"Dear children, this Christmas Satan wanted in a special way to spoil God's plans. You, dear children, have discerned Satan even on Christmas Day itself. But God is winning in all your hearts. So let your hearts keep on being happy. Thank you for having responded to my call."

January 3, 1985

"Dear children, these days the Lord has bestowed upon you great graces. Let this week be one of thanksgiving for all the graces God has granted you. Thank you for having responded to my call."

January 10, 1985

"Dear children, today I want to thank you for all your sacrifices but special thanks to those who have become dear to my heart and come here gladly. There are enough parishioners who are not listening to the messages, but because of those who are in a special way close to my heart, because of them I am giving messages for the parish. And I will go on giving them because I love you and I want you to spread my messages with your heart. Thank you for having responded to my call."

January 17, 1985

"Dear children, these days Satan is working underhandedly against this parish, and you, dear children, have fallen asleep in prayer and only some are going to Mass. Withstand the days of temptation! Thank you for having responded to my call."

January 24, 1985

"Dear children, these days you have experienced God's sweetness through the renewals which have been in this parish. Satan wants to work still more fiercely to take away your joy from each one of you. By prayer you can completely disarm him and ensure your happiness. Thank you for having responded to my call."

January 31, 1985

"Dear children, today I wish to tell you to open your hearts to God like the spring flowers which crave for the sun. I am your Mother and I always want you to be closer to the Father and that He will always give abundant gifts to your hearts. Thank you for having responded to my call."

February 7, 1985

"Dear children, these days Satan is manifesting himself in a special way in this parish. Pray, dear children, that God's plan is brought into effect and that every work of Satan ends up for the glory of God. I have stayed with you this long so I might help you along in your trials. Thank you for having responded to my call."

February 14, 1985

"Dear children, today is the day when I give you a message for the parish, but the whole parish is not accepting the messages and is not living them. I am saddened and I want you, dear children, to listen to me and to live my messages. Every family must pray family prayer and read the Bible! Thank you for having responded to my call."

February 21, 1985

"Dear children, from day to day I have been inviting you to renewal and prayer in the parish, but you are not accepting it. Today I am calling you for the last time! Now it's Lent and you as a parish can turn to my message during Lent out of love. If you don't do that, I don't wish to keep on giving messages. God is permitting me that. Thank you for having responded to my call."

February 28, 1985

"Dear children, today I call you to live the word this week: 'I love God!' Dear children, through love you will achieve everything and even what you think is impossible. God wants this parish to belong completely to Him. And that's what I want too. Thank you for having responded to my call."

March 7, 1985

"Dear children, today I call you to renew prayer in your families. Dear children, encourage the very young to prayer and the children to go to Holy Mass. Thank you for having responded to my call."

March 14, 1985

"Dear children, in your life you have all experienced light and darkness. God grants to every person to recognize good and evil. I am calling you to the light, which you should carry to all the people who are in darkness. People who are in darkness daily come into your homes. Dear children, give them the light! Thank you for having responded to my call."

March 21, 1985

"Dear children, I wish to keep on giving messages and, therefore, today I call you to live and accept my messages!

Dear children, I love you and in a special way I have chosen this parish, one more dear to me than the others, in which I have gladly remained when the Almighty sent me. Therefore, I call on you - accept me, dear children, that it might go well with you. Listen to my messages Thank you for having responded to my call."

March 28, 1985

"Dear children, today I wish to call you to pray, pray, pray! In prayer you shall perceive the greatest joy and the way out of every situation that has no exit. Thank you for starting up prayer. Each individual is dear to my heart. And I thank all who have urged prayer in their families. Thank you for having responded to my call."

April 4, 1985 (HOLY THURSDAY)

"Dear children, I thank you for having started to think more about God's glory in your hearts. Today is the day when I wished to stop giving the messages because some individuals did not accept me. The parish has been moved and I wish to keep on giving you messages as it has never been in history from the beginning of the world. Thank you for having responded to my call."

April 11, 1985

"Dear children, today I wish to say to everyone in the parish to pray in a special way to the Holy Spirit for enlightenment. From today God wants to test the parish in a special way in order that He might strengthen it in faith. Thank you for having responded to my call."

April 18, 1985

"Dear children, today I thank you for every opening of your hearts. Joy overtakes me for every heart that is opened to

God especially from the parish. Rejoice with me! Pray all the prayers for the opening of sinful hearts. I desire that. God desires that through me. Thank you for having responded to my call."

April 25, 1985

"Dear children, today I want to tell you to begin to work in your hearts as you are working in the fields. Work and change your hearts so that a new spirit from God can take its place in your hearts. Thank you for having responded to my call."

May 2, 1985

"Dear children, today I call you to prayer with the heart, and not just from habit. Some are coming but do not wish to move ahead in prayer. Therefore, I wish to warn you like a Mother. Pray that prayer prevails in your hearts in every moment. Thank you for having responded to my call."

May 9, 1985

"Dear children, no, you do not know how many graces God is giving you. You do not want to move ahead during these days when the Holy Spirit is working in a special way. Your hearts are turned toward the things of earth and they preoccupy you. Turn your hearts toward prayer and seek the Holy Spirit to be poured out on you. Thank you for having responded to my call."

May 16, 1985

"Dear children, I am calling you to a more active prayer and attendance at Holy Mass. I wish your Mass to be an experience of God. I wish especially to say to the young people: be open to the Holy Spirit because God wishes to draw you to Himself in these days when Satan is at work. Thank you for having responded to my call."

May 23, 1985

"Dear children, these days I call you especially to open your hearts to the Holy Spirit. Especially during these days the Holy Spirit is working through you. Open your hearts and surrender your lives to Jesus so that He works through your hearts and strengthens you in faith. Thank you for having responded to my call."

May 30, 1985

"Dear children, I call you again to prayer with the heart. Let prayer, dear children, be your everyday food in a special way when your work in the fields is so wearing you out that you cannot pray with the heart. Pray, and then you shall overcome even every weariness. Prayer will be your joy and your rest. Thank you for having responded to my call."

June 6, 1985

"Dear children, during these days people from all nations will be coming into the parish. And now I am calling you to love: love first of all your own household members, and then you will be able to accept and love all who are coming. Thank you for having responded to my call."

June 13, 1985

"Dear children, until the anniversary day I am calling you, the parish, to pray more and to let your prayer be a sign of surrender to God. Dear children, I know that you are all tired, but you don't know how to surrender yourselves to me. During these days surrender yourselves completely to me! Thank you for having responded to my call."

June 20, 1985

"Dear children, for this Feast Day I wish to tell you to open your hearts to the Master of all hearts. Give me all your feelings and all your problems! I wish to comfort you in all your trials. I wish to fill you with peace, joy, and love of God. Thank you for having responded to my call."

June 28, 1985 (FRIDAY)

"Dear children, today I am giving you a message through which I desire to call you to humility. These days you have felt great joy because of all the people who have come and to whom you could tell your experiences with love. Now I invite you to continue in humility and with an open heart, speak to all those who are coming. Thank you for having responded to my message."

July 4, 1985

"Dear children, I thank you for every sacrifice you have offered. And now I urge you to offer every sacrifice with love. I wish you, the helpless ones, to begin helping with confidence and the Lord will keep on giving to you in confidence. Thank you for having responded to my call."

July 11, 1985

"Dear children, I love the parish and with my mantle I protect it from every work of Satan. Pray that Satan retreats from the parish and from every individual who comes into the parish. In that way you shall be able to hear every call of God and answer it with your life. Thank you for having responded to my call."

July 18, 1985

"Dear children, today I call you to place more blessed objects in your homes and call everyone to put some blessed object on their person. Bless all the objects and thus Satan will attack you less because you will have armor against him. Thank you for having responded to my call."

July 25, 1985

"Dear children, I desire to lead you, but you do not want to listen to the messages. Today I am calling you to listen to my messages and then you will be able to live everything that God tells me to convey to you. Open yourselves to God and God will work through you and keep on giving you everything you need. Thank you for having responded to my call."

August 1, 1985

"Dear children, I wish to tell you that I have chosen this parish and that I am guarding it in my hands like a little flower that does not want to die. I call you to surrender to me so that I can keep on presenting you to God, fresh and without sin. Satan has taken part of the plan and wants to possess it. Pray that he does not succeed in that, because I wish you for myself so I can keep on giving you to God. Thank you for having responded to my call."

August 8, 1985

"Dear children, today I call you especially now to advance against Satan by means of prayer. Satan wants to work still more now that you know he is at work. Dear children, put on the armor for battle and with the Rosary in your hand, defeat him! Thank you for having responded to my call."

August 15, 1985 (THE ASSUMPTION)

> **"Dear children, today I am blessing you and I wish to tell you that I love you and that I urge you to live my messages. Today I am blessing you with the solemn blessing that the Almighty grants me. Thank you for having responded to my call."**

August 22, 1985

> **"Dear children, today I wish to tell you that God wants to send you trials which you can overcome by prayer. God is testing you through daily chores. Now pray to peacefully withstand every trial. From everything through which God tests you, come out more open to God and approach Him with love. Thank you for having responded to my call."**

August 29, 1985

This message has a spiritual meaning.

> **"Dear children, I am calling you to prayer, especially since Satan wishes to take advantage of the yield of your vineyards. Pray that Satan does not succeed in his plan. Thank you for your response to my call."**

September 5, 1985

> **"Dear children, today I thank you for all the prayers. Keep on praying all the more so that Satan will be far away from this place. Dear children, Satan's plan has failed. Pray for the fulfillment of what God plans in this parish. I especially thank the young people for the sacrifices they have offered up. Thank you for having responded to my call."**

September 12, 1985

This message was given to Marija before the celebration of the Feast of the Holy Cross which was the day of the largest pilgrimage of the year at Krizevac:

"Dear children, I want to tell you that the cross should be central these days. Pray especially before the crucifix from which great graces are coming. Now in your homes make a special consecration to the crucifix. Promise that you will neither offend Jesus nor abuse the crucifix. Thank you for having responded to my call."

September 19, 1985

No message was given by Our Lady.

September 20, 1985 (FRIDAY)

"Dear children, today I invite you to live in humility all the messages which I am giving you. Do not become arrogant living the messages and saying, 'I am living the messages.' If you shall bear and live the messages in your heart, everyone will feel it so that words, which serve those who do not obey, will not be necessary. For you, dear children, it is necessary to live and witness by your lives. Thank you for having responded to my call."

September 26, 1985

"Dear children, I thank you for all the prayers. Thank you for all the sacrifices. I wish to tell you, dear children, to renew the messages which I am giving you. Especially live the fast, because by fasting you will achieve and cause me the joy of the whole plan, which God is planning here in Medjugorje, being fulfilled. Thank you for having responded to my call."

October 3, 1985

"Dear children, I wish to tell you to thank God for all the graces which God has given you. For all the fruits thank the Lord and glorify Him! Dear children, learn to give thanks in little things and then you will be able to give thanks also for the big things. Thank you for having responded to my call."

October 10, 1985

"Dear children, I wish also today to call you to live the messages in the parish. Especially I wish to call the youth of the parish, who are dear to me. Dear children, if you live the messages, you are living the seed of holiness. I, as the Mother, wish to call you all to holiness so that you can bestow it on others. You are a mirror to others! Thank you for having responded to my call."

October 17, 1985

"Dear children, everything has its own time. Today I call you to start working on your hearts. Now that all the work in the fields is over, you are finding time for cleaning even the most neglected areas, but you leave your heart aside. Work more and clean with love every part of your heart. Thank you for having responded to my call."

October 24, 1985

"Dear children, from day to day I wish to clothe you in holiness, goodness, obedience, and God's love, so that from day to day you become more beautiful and more prepared for your Master. Dear children, listen to and live my messages. I wish to guide you. Thank you for having responded to my call."

October 31, 1985

"Dear children, today I wish to call you to work in the Church. I love all the same and I desire from each one to work as much as possible. I know, dear children, that you can, but you do not wish to because you feel small and humble in these things. You need to be courageous and with little flowers do your share for the Church and for Jesus so that everyone can be satisfied. Thank you for having responded to my call."

November 7, 1985

"Dear children, I am calling you to the love of neighbor and love toward the one from whom evil comes to you. In that way you will be able to discern the intentions of hearts. Pray and love, dear children! By love you are able to do even that which you think is impossible. Thank you for having responded to my call."

November 14, 1985

"Dear children, I, your Mother, love you and wish to urge you to prayer. I am tireless, dear children, and I am calling you even then, when you are far away from my heart. I am a Mother, and even though I feel pain for each one who goes astray, I forgive easily and am happy for every child who returns to me. Thank you for having responded to my call."

November 21, 1985

"Dear children, I want to tell you that this season is especially for you from the parish. When it was summer, you saw that you had a lot of work. Now you don't have work in the fields, work on your own self personally! Come to Mass because this is the season given to you. Dear children, there are enough of those who come regularly despite bad weather, because they love me and want to show their love in a special way. What I want from you is to show me your love by coming to Mass, and the Lord will reward you abundantly. Thank you for having responded to my call."

November 28, 1985

"Dear children, I want to thank everyone for all you have done for me, especially the youth. I beseech you, dear children, come to prayer with awareness. In prayer you shall come to know the greatness of God. Thank you for having responded to my call."

December 5, 1985

"Dear children, I am calling you to prepare yourselves for Christmas by means of penance, prayer, and works of charity. Dear children, do not look toward material things, because then you will not be able to experience Christmas. Thank you for having responded to my call."

December 12, 1985

"Dear children, for Christmas my invitation is that together we glorify Jesus. I present Him to you in a special way on that day and my invitation to you is that on that day we glorify Jesus and His nativity. Dear children, on that day pray still more and think more about Jesus. Thank you for having responded to my call."

December 19, 1985

"Dear children, today I wish to call you to love of neighbor. The more you will to love your neighbor, the more you shall experience Jesus especially on Christmas Day. God will bestow great gifts on you if you surrender yourselves to Him. I wish in a special way on Christmas Day to give mothers my own Special Motherly Blessing and Jesus will bless the rest with His own blessing. Thank you for having responded to my call."

December 25, 1985 (CHRISTMAS - SPECIAL BLESSING)

Our Lady gives a Special Motherly Blessing to mothers and Jesus
blesses the rest. [See the weekly message of December 19, 1985.]

December 26, 1985

"Dear children, I wish to thank all who have listened to my
messages and who on Christmas Day have lived what I said.
Undefiled by sin from now on, I wish to lead you further in
love. Abandon your hearts to me! Thank you for having
responded to my call."

January 2, 1986

"Dear children, I invite you to decide completely for God. I
beseech you, dear children, to surrender yourselves completely
and you shall be able to live everything I am telling you. It
shall not be difficult for you to surrender yourselves
completely to God. Thank you for having responded to my
call."

January 9, 1986

"Dear children, I invite you by your prayers to help Jesus
along in the fulfillment of all of the plans which He is forming
here.   And offer your sacrifices to Jesus in order that
everything is fulfilled the way He has planned it and that
Satan can accomplish nothing.   Thank you for having
responded to my call."

January 16, 1986

"Dear children, today also I am calling you to prayer. Your
prayers are necessary to me so that God may be glorified
through all of you. Dear children, I pray you, obey and live
the Mother's invitation, because only out of love am I calling

you in order that I might help you. Thank you for having responded to my call."

January 23, 1986

"Dear children, again I call you to prayer with the heart. If you pray with the heart, dear children, the ice of your brothers' hearts will melt and every barrier shall disappear. Conversion will be easy for all who desire to accept it. You must pray for this gift which by prayer you must obtain for your neighbor. Thank you for having responded to my call."

January 30, 1986

"Dear children, today I call you to pray that God's plans for us may be realized and also everything that God desires through you! Help others to be converted, especially those who are coming to Medjugorje. Dear children, do not allow Satan to get control of your hearts, so you would be an image of Satan and not of me. I call you to pray for how you might be witnesses of my presence. Without you, God cannot bring to reality that which He desires. God has given a free will to everyone, and it's in your control. Thank you for having responded to my call."

February 6, 1986

"Dear children, this parish, which I have chosen, is special and different from others. And I am giving great graces to all who pray with the heart. Dear children, I am giving messages first of all to the residents of the parish, and then to all the others. First of all you must accept the messages, and then the others. You shall be answerable to me and to my Son, Jesus. Thank you for having responded to my call."

February 13, 1986

"Dear children, this Lent is a special incentive for you to change. Start from this moment. Turn off the television and renounce various things that are of no value. Dear children, I am calling you individually to conversion. This season is for you. Thank you for having responded to my call."

February 20, 1986

"Dear children, the second message of these Lenten days is that you renew prayer before the crucifix. Dear children, I am giving you special graces and Jesus is giving you special gifts from the Crucifix. Take them and live! Reflect on Jesus' Passion and in your life be united with Jesus! Thank you for having responded to my call."

February 27, 1986

"Dear children, in humility live the messages which I am giving you. Thank you for having responded to my call."

March 6, 1986

"Dear children, today I call you to open yourselves more to God, so that He can work through you. The more you open yourselves, the more you receive the fruits. I wish to call you again to prayer. Thank you for having responded to my call."

March 13, 1986

"Dear children, today I call you to live this Lent by means of your little sacrifices. Thank you for every sacrifice you have brought me. Dear children, live that way continuously, and with your love help me to present the sacrifice. God will reward you for that. Thank you for having responded to my call."

March 20, 1986

"Dear children, Today I call you to approach prayer actively.
You wish to live everything I am telling you, but you are not
succeeding because you are not praying. Dear children, I
beseech you to open yourselves and begin to pray. Prayer will
be your joy. If you make a start, it won't be boring to you
because you will be praying out of joy. Thank you for having
responded to my call."

March 27, 1986

"Dear children, I wish to thank you for all the sacrifices and
I invite you to the greatest sacrifice, the sacrifice of love.
Without love, you are not able to accept either me or my Son.
Without love, you cannot give an account of your experiences
to others. Therefore, dear children, I call you to begin to live
love within yourselves. Thank you for having responded to
my call."

April 3, 1986

"Dear children, I wish to call you to a living of the Holy Mass.
There are many of you who have sensed the beauty of the Holy
Mass, but there are also those who come unwillingly. I have
chosen you, dear children, but Jesus gives you His graces in
the Mass. Therefore, consciously live the Holy Mass and let
your coming to it be a joyful one. Come to it with love and
make the Mass your own. Thank you for having responded to
my call."

April 10, 1986

"Dear children, I desire to call you to grow in love. A flower
is not able to grow normally without water. So also you, dear
children, are not able to grow without God's blessing. From
day to day you need to seek His blessing so you will grow

normally and perform all your actions in union with God. Thank you for having responded to my call."

April 17, 1986

"Dear children, you are absorbed with materials things, but in the material you lose everything that God wishes to give you. I call you, dear children, to pray for the gifts of the Holy Spirit which are necessary for you now in order to be able to give witness to my presence here and to all that I am giving you. Dear children, surrender to me so I can lead you completely. Don't be absorbed with material things. Thank you for having responded to my call."

April 24, 1986

"Dear children, today my invitation is that you pray. Dear children, you are forgetting that you are all important. The elderly are especially important in the family. Urge them to pray. Let all the young people be an example to others by their lives and let them witness to Jesus. Dear children, I beseech you, begin to change through prayer and you will know what you need to do. Thank you for having responded to my call."

May 1, 1986

"Dear children, I beseech you to start changing your life in the family. Let the family be a harmonious flower that I wish to give to Jesus. Dear children, let every family be active in prayer for I wish that the fruits in the family be seen one day. Only that way shall I give all, like petals, as a gift to Jesus in fulfillment of God's plan. Thank you for having responded to my call."

May 8, 1986

"Dear children, you are the ones responsible for the messages. The source of grace is here, but you, dear children, are the vessels which transport the gifts. Therefore, dear children, I am calling you to do your job with responsibility. Each one shall be responsible according to his own ability. Dear children, I am calling you to give the gifts to others with love, and not to keep them for yourselves. Thank you for having responded to my call."

May 15, 1986

"Dear children, today I call you to give me your heart so I can change it to be like mine. You are wondering, dear children, why you cannot respond to that which I am seeking from you. You are not able to because you have not given me your heart so I can change it. You are talking but you are not doing. I call on you to do everything that I am telling you. That way I will be with you. Thank you for having responded to my call."

May 22, 1986

"Dear children, today I wish to give you my own love. You do not know , dear children, how great my love is, and you do not know how to accept it. In various ways I wish to show it to you, but you, dear children, do not recognize it. You do not understand my words with your heart and neither are you able to comprehend my love. Dear children, accept me in your life so you will be able to accept all I am saying to you and to which I am calling you. Thank you for having responded to my call."

May 29, 1986

"Dear children, today my call to you is that in your life you live love towards God and neighbor. Without love, dear children, you can do nothing. Therefore, dear children, I am calling you to live in mutual love. Only in that way will you be able to love and accept both me and all those around you who are coming into your parish. Everyone will sense my love through you. Therefore, I beseech you, dear children, to start loving from today with an ardent love, the love with which I love you. Thank you for having responded to my call."

June 5, 1986

"Dear children, today I am calling on you to decide whether or not you wish to live the messages which I am giving you. I wish you to be active in living and spreading the messages. Especially, dear children, I wish that you all be the reflection of Jesus, which will enlighten this unfaithful world walking in darkness. I wish all of you to be the light for everyone and that you give witness in the light. Dear children, you are not called to the darkness, but you are called to the light. Therefore, live the light with your own life. Thank you for having responded to my call."

June 12, 1986

"Dear children, today I call you to begin to pray the Rosary with a living faith. That way I will be able to help you. You, dear children, wish to obtain graces, but you are not praying. I am not able to help you because you do not want to get started. Dear children, I am calling you to pray the Rosary and that your Rosary be an obligation which you shall fulfill with joy. That way you shall understand the reason I am with you this long. I desire to teach you to pray. Thank you for having responded to my call."

June 19, 1986

"Dear children, during these days my Lord is allowing me to be able to intercede for more graces for you. Therefore, I wish to urge you once more to pray, dear children! Pray without ceasing! That way I will give you the joy which the Lord gives to me. With these graces, dear children, I want your sufferings to be a joy. I am your Mother and I desire to help you. Thank you for having responded to my call."

June 26, 1986

"Dear children, God is allowing me along with Himself to bring about this oasis of peace. I wish to call on you to protect it and that the oasis always be unspoiled. There are those who by their carelessness are destroying the peace and the prayer. I am inviting you to give witness and by your life to help to preserve the peace. Thank you for having responded to my call."

July 3, 1986

"Dear children, today I am calling you all to prayer. Without prayer, dear children, you are not able to experience either God or me or the graces which I am giving you. Therefore, my call to you is that the beginning and end of your day always be prayer. Dear children, I wish to lead you daily more and more in prayer, but you are not able to grow because you do not desire it. My call, dear children, is that for you prayer be in the first place. Thank you for having responded to my call."

July 10, 1986

"Dear children, today I am calling you to holiness. Without holiness you cannot live. Therefore, with love overcome every sin and with love overcome all the difficulties which are coming to you. Dear children, I beseech you to live love within yourselves. Thank you for having responded to my call."

July 17, 1986

"Dear children, today I am calling you to reflect upon why I am with you this long. I am the Mediatrix between you and God. Therefore, dear children, I desire to call you to live always out of love all that which God desires of you. For that reason, dear children, in your own humility live all the messages which I am giving you. Thank you for having responded to my call."

July 24, 1986

"Dear children, I rejoice because of all of you who are on the way of holiness and I beseech you, by your own testimony help those who do not know how to live in holiness. Therefore, dear children, let your family be a place where holiness is born. Help everyone to live in holiness, but especially your own family. Thank you for having responded to my call."

July 31, 1986

"Dear children, hatred gives birth to dissensions and does not regard anyone or anything. I call you always to bring harmony and peace. Especially, dear children, in the place where you live, act with love. Let your only instrument always be love. By love turn everything into good which Satan desires to destroy and possess. Only that way will you be completely mine and I shall be able to help you. Thank you for having responded to my call."

August 7, 1986

"Dear children, you know that I promised you an oasis of peace, but you don't know that beside an oasis stands the desert, where Satan is lurking and wants to tempt each one of you. Dear children, only by prayer are you able to overcome every influence of Satan in your place. I am with you, but I cannot take away your freedom. Thank you for having responded to my call."

August 14, 1986

"Dear children, my call to you is that your prayer be the joy of an
encounter with the Lord. I am not able to guide you as long as
you yourselves do not experience joy in prayer! From day to day
I desire to lead you more and more in prayer, but I do not wish
to force you. Thank you for having responded to my call."

August 21, 1986

"Dear children, I thank you for the love which you are showing
me. You know, dear children, that I love you immeasurably,
and daily I pray the Lord to help you to understand the love
which I am showing you. Therefore, you, dear children, pray,
pray, pray!"

August 28, 1986

"Dear children, my call is that in everything you would be an
image for others, especially in prayer and witnessing. Dear
children, without you I am not able to help the world. I desire
that you cooperate with me in everything, even in the smallest
things. Therefore, dear children, help me by letting your
prayer be from the heart and all of you surrendering
completely to me. That way I shall be able to teach and lead
you on this way which I have begun with you. Thank you for
having responded to my call."

September 4, 1986

"Dear children, today again I am calling you to prayer and
fasting. You know, dear children, that with your help I am
able to accomplish everything and force Satan not to be
seducing you to evil and to remove himself from this place.
Dear children, Satan is lurking for each individual. Especially
in everyday affairs, he wants to spread confusion among each
one of you. Therefore, dear children, my call to you is that

your day would be only prayer and complete surrender to God. Thank you for having responded to my call."

September 11, 1986

"Dear children, for these days while you are joyfully celebrating the cross, I desire that your cross also would be a joy for you. Especially, dear children, pray that you may be able to accept sickness and suffering with love the way Jesus accepted them. Only that way shall I be able with joy to give out to you the graces and healings which Jesus is permitting me. Thank you for having responded to my call."

September 18, 1986

"Dear children, today again I thank you for all that you have accomplished for me in these days. Especially, dear children, I thank you in the name of Jesus for the sacrifices which you offered during this past week. Dear children, you are forgetting that I desire sacrifices from you so I can help you and to drive Satan away from you. Therefore, I am calling you again to offer sacrifices with a special reverence toward God. Thank you for having responded to my call."

September 25, 1986

"Dear children, by your own peace I am calling you to help others to see and begin to seek peace. You, dear children, are at peace and not able to comprehend non-peace. Therefore, I am calling you, so that by your prayer and your life you help to destroy everything that's evil in people and uncover the deception that Satan makes use of. You pray that the truth prevails in all hearts. Thank you for having responded to my call."

October 2, 1986

"Dear children, today again I am calling you to pray. You, dear children, are not able to understand how great the value of prayer is as long as you yourselves do not say: 'now is the time for prayer, now nothing else is important to me, now not one person is important to me but God.' Dear children, consecrate yourselves to prayer with special love so that God will be able to render graces back to you. Thank you for having responded to my call."

October 9, 1986

"Dear children, you know that I desire to lead you on the way of holiness, but I do not want to compel you to be saints by force. I desire that each of you by your own little self-denials help yourself and me so I can lead you from day to day to holiness. Therefore, dear children, I do not desire to force you to observe the messages. But rather this long time that I am with you is a sign that I love you immeasurably, and what I desire of each individual is to become holy. Thank you for having responded to my call."

October 16, 1986

"Dear children, today again I want to show you how much I love you, but I am sorry that I am not able to help each one to understand my love. Therefore, dear children, I am calling you to prayer and complete surrender to God, because Satan wants to sift you through everyday affairs and in your life he wants to snatch the first place. Therefore, dear children, pray without ceasing! Thank you for having responded to my call."

October 23, 1986

"Dear children, today again I call you to pray. Especially, dear children, do I call you to pray for peace. Without your prayers, dear children, I cannot help you to fulfill the message which the Lord has given me to give to you. Therefore, dear children, pray, so that in prayer you realize what God is giving you. Thank you for having responded to my call."

October 30, 1986

"Dear children, today again I desire to call you to take seriously and carry out the messages which I am giving you. Dear children, it is for your sake that I have stayed this long so I could help you to fulfill all the messages which I am giving you. Therefore, dear children, out of love for me carry out all the messages which I am giving you. Thank you for having responded to my call."

November 6, 1986

"Dear children, today I wish to call you to pray daily for the souls in purgatory. For every soul prayer and grace is necessary to reach God and the love of God. By doing this, dear children, you obtain new intercessors who will help you in life to realize that all the earthly things are not important for you, that only Heaven is that for which it is necessary to strive. Therefore, dear children, pray without ceasing that you may be able to help yourselves and the others to whom your prayers will bring joy. Thank you for having responded to my call."

November 13, 1986

"Dear children, today again I am calling you to pray with your whole heart and day by day to change your life. Especially, dear children, I am calling that by your prayers and sacrifices you begin to live in holiness, because I desire that each one of you who has been to this fountain of grace will come to Paradise with the special gift which you shall give me, and that is holiness. Therefore, dear children, pray and daily change your life in order to become holy. I shall always be close to you. Thank you for having responded to my call."

November 20, 1986

"Dear children, today also I am calling you to live and follow with a special love all the messages which I am giving you. Dear children, God does not want you lukewarm and undecided, but that you totally surrender to Him. You know that I love you and that I burn out of love for you. Therefore, dear children, you also decide for love so that you will burn out of love and daily experience God's love. Dear children, decide for love so that love prevails in all of you, but not human love, rather God's love. Thank you for having responded to my call."

November 27, 1986

"Dear children, again today I call you to consecrate your life to me with love, so I am able to guide you with love. I love you, dear children, with a special love and I desire to bring you all to heaven unto God. I want you to realize that this life lasts briefly compared to the one in heaven. Therefore, dear children, decide again for God. Only that way will I be able to show how much you are dear to me and how much I desire all to be saved and to be with me in Heaven. Thank you for having responded to my call."

December 4, 1986

"Dear children, today I call you to prepare your hearts for these days when the Lord particularly desires to purify you from all the sins of your past. You, dear children, are not able by yourselves, therefore, I am here to help you. You pray, dear children! Only that way shall you be able to recognize all the evil that is in you and surrender it to the Lord so the Lord may completely purify your hearts. Therefore, dear children, pray without ceasing and prepare your hearts in penance and fasting. Thank you for having responded to my call."

December 11, 1986

"Dear children, I am calling you to pray especially at this time in order to experience the joy of meeting with the newborn Jesus. Dear children, I desire that you experience these days just as I experienced them. With joy I wish to guide you and show you the joy into which I desire to bring each one of you. Therefore, dear children, pray and surrender completely to me. Thank you for having responded to my call."

December 18, 1986

"Dear children, once again I desire to call you to prayer. When you pray, you are much more beautiful, like flowers which, after the snow, show all their beauty and all their colors become indescribable. So also you, dear children, after prayer show more before God all that is beautiful to please Him. Therefore, dear children, pray and open your inner self to the Lord so that He makes of you a harmonious and beautiful flower for Paradise. Thank you for having responded to my call."

December 25, 1986 (CHRISTMAS DAY)

"Dear children, today also I give thanks to the Lord for all that He is doing for me, especially for this gift that I am able to be with you also today. Dear children, these are the days in which the Father grants special graces to all who open their hearts. I bless you and I desire that you too, dear children, become alive to the graces and place everything at Gods' disposal so that He may be glorified through you. My heart carefully follows your steps. Thank you for having responded to my call."

January 1, 1987

"Dear children, today I wish to call on all of you that in the New Year you live the messages which I am giving you. Dear children, you know that for your sake I have remained a long time so I might teach you how to make progress on the way of holiness. Therefore, dear children, pray without ceasing and live the messages which I am giving you for I am doing it with great love toward God and toward you. Thank you for having responded to my call."

January 8, 1987

"Dear children, I desire to thank you for every response to the messages. Especially, dear children, thank you for all the sacrifices and prayers which you have presented to me. Dear children, I desire to keep on giving you still further messages, only not every Thursday, dear children, but on the 25th of each month. The time has come when what my Lord desired has been fulfilled. Now I will give you fewer messages but I am still with you. Therefore, dear children, I beseech you, listen to my messages and live them, so I can guide you. Dear children, thank you for having responded to my call."

CHAPTER 3

THE MONTHLY MESSAGES
OF OUR LADY
THROUGH MARIJA

(January 25, 1987 to June 25, 1991)

"I GIVE YOU MY SPECIAL BLESSING." **(December 25, 1988)**

On January 8, 1987, Our Lady announced Her desire to continue giving messages, however, not weekly but rather monthly, on the twenty-fifth of each month.

January 25, 1987

"Dear children, behold, also today I want to call you to start living a new life as of today. Dear children, I want you to comprehend that God has chosen each one of you, in order to use you in a great plan for the salvation of mankind. You are not able to comprehend how great your role is in God's design. Therefore, dear children, pray so that in prayer you may be able to comprehend what God's plan is in your regard. I am with you in order that you may be able to bring it about in all its fullness. Thank you for having responded to my call."

February 25, 1987

"Dear children, today I want to wrap you all in my mantle and lead you all along the way of conversion. Dear children, I beseech you, surrender to the Lord your entire past, all the evil that has accumulated in your hearts. I want each one of you to be happy, but in sin nobody can be happy. Therefore, dear children, pray, and in prayer you shall realize a new way of joy. Joy will manifest in your hearts and thus you shall be joyful witnesses of that which I and My Son want from each one of you. I am blessing you. Thank you for having responded to my call."

March 25, 1987 (SPECIAL BLESSING)

"Dear children, today I am grateful to you for your presence in this place, where I am giving you special graces. I call each one of you to begin to live as of today that life which God wishes of you and to begin to perform good works of love and mercy. I do not want you, dear children, to live the message and be committing sin which is displeasing to me. Therefore, dear children, I want each of you to live a new life without the murder* of all that God produces in you and is giving you. I give you my Special Blessing and I am remaining with you on your way of conversion. Thank you for having responded to my call."

* "Murder" rather than "destroy" was chosen for the translation of the Croatian word, "ubijanje," because Our Lady used a very strong word meaning to kill something living. An automobile as well as a human being can be destroyed. The purest translation is "murder."

April 25, 1987

"Dear children, today also I am calling you to prayer. You know, dear children, that God grants special graces in prayer. Therefore, seek and pray in order that you may be able to comprehend all that I am giving here. I call you, dear children, to prayer with the heart. You know that without prayer you cannot comprehend all that God is planning through each one of you. Therefore, pray! I desire that through each one of you God's plan may be fulfilled, that all which God has planted in your heart may keep on growing. So pray that God's blessing may protect each one of you from all the evil that is threatening you. I bless you, dear children. Thank you for having responded to my call."

May 25, 1987

"Dear children, I am calling everyone of you to start living in God's love. Dear children, you are ready to commit sin, and to put yourselves in the hands of Satan without reflecting. I call on each one of you to consciously decide for God and against Satan. I am your Mother and, therefore, I want to lead you all to complete holiness. I want each one of you to be happy here on earth and to be with me in Heaven. That is, dear children, the purpose of my coming here and it's my desire. Thank you for having responded to my call."

June 25, 1987 (SPECIAL BLESSING)

"Dear children, today I thank you and I want to invite you all to God's peace. I want each one of you to experience in your heart that peace which God gives. I want to bless you all today. I am blessing you with God's Blessing and I beseech you, dear children, to follow and to live my way. I love you, dear children, and so not even counting the number of times, I go on calling you and I thank you for all that you are doing for my intentions. I beg you, help me to present you to God and to save you. Thank you for having responded to my call."

July 25, 1987

"Dear children, I beseech you to take up the way of holiness beginning today. I love you and, therefore, I want you to be holy. I do not want Satan to block you on that way. Dear children, pray and accept all that God is offering you on a way which is bitter. But at the same time, God will reveal every sweetness to whomever begins to go on that way, and He will gladly answer every call of God. Do not attribute importance to petty things. Long for heaven. Thank you for having responded to my call."

August 25, 1987

"Dear children, today also I am calling you all in order that each one of you decides to live my messages. God has permitted me also in this year, which the Church has dedicated to me, to be able to speak to you and to be able to spur you on to holiness. Dear children, seek from God the graces which He is giving you through me. I am ready to intercede with God for all that you seek so that your holiness may be complete. Therefore, dear children, do not forget to seek, because God has permitted me to obtain graces for you. Thank you for having responded to my call."

September 25, 1987

"Dear children, today also I want to call you all to prayer. Let prayer be your life. Dear children, dedicate your time only to Jesus and He will give you everything that you are seeking. He will reveal Himself to you in fullness. Dear children, Satan is strong and is waiting to test each one of you. Pray, and that way he will neither be able to injure you nor block you on the way of holiness. Dear children, through prayer grow all the more toward God from day to day. Thank you for having responded to my call."

October 25, 1987

"My dear children, today I want to call all of you to decide for Paradise. The way is difficult for those who have not decided for God. Dear children, decide and believe that God is offering Himself to you in His fullness. You are invited and you need to answer the call of the Father, who is calling you through me. Pray, because in prayer each one of you will be able to achieve complete love. I am blessing you and I desire to help you so that each one of you might be under my motherly mantle. Thank you for having responded to my call."

November 25, 1987

"Dear children, today also I call each one of you to decide to surrender again everything completely to me. Only that way will I be able to present each of you to God. Dear children, you know that I love you immeasurably and that I desire each of you for myself, but God has given to all a freedom which I lovingly respect and humbly submit to. I desire, dear children, that you help so that everything God has planned in this parish shall be realized. If you do not pray, you shall not be able to recognize my love and the plans which God has for this parish and for each individual. Pray that Satan does not entice you with his pride and deceptive strength. I am with you and I want you to believe me, that I love you. Thank you for having responded to my call."

December 25, 1987

"Dear children, rejoice with me! My heart is rejoicing because of Jesus and today I want to give Him to you. Dear children, I want each one of you to open your heart to Jesus and I will give Him to you with love. Dear children, I want Him to change you, to teach you, and to protect you. Today I am praying in a special way for each one of you and I am presenting you to God so He will manifest Himself in you. I am calling you to sincere prayer with the heart so that every prayer of yours may be an encounter with God. In your work and in your everyday life, put God in the first place. I call you today with great seriousness to obey me and to do as I am calling you. Thank you for having responded to my call."

January 25, 1988

"Dear children, today again I am calling you to complete conversion, which is difficult for those who have not chosen God. I am calling you, dear children, to convert fully to God. God can give you everything that you seek from Him. But you seek God only when sicknesses, problems, and difficulties come

to you and you think that God is far from you and is not
listening and does not hear your prayers. No, dear children,
that is not the truth! When you are far from God, you cannot
receive graces because you do not seek them with a firm faith.
Day by day, I am praying for you and I want to draw you ever
closer to God; but I cannot if you don't want it. Therefore,
dear children, put your life in God's hands. I bless you all.
Thank you for having responded to my call."

February 25, 1988

"Dear children, today again I am calling you to prayer and
complete surrender to God. You know that I love you and am
coming here out of love, so I could show you the path of peace
and salvation for your souls. I want you to obey me and not
permit Satan to seduce you. Dear children, Satan is very
strong and, therefore, I ask you to dedicate your prayers to me
so that those who are under his influence may be saved. Give
witness by your life, sacrifice your lives for the salvation of the
world. I am with you and I am grateful to you, but in heaven
you shall receive the Father's reward which He has promised
you. Therefore, little children, do not be afraid. If you pray,
Satan cannot injure you even a little, because you are God's
children and He is watching over you. Pray, and let the
Rosary always be in your hands as a sign to Satan that you
belong to me. Thank you for having responded to my call."

March 25, 1988

"Dear children, today also I am calling you to a complete
surrender to God. You, dear children, are not conscious of
how God loves you with such a great love. Because of it He
permits me to be with you so I can instruct you and help you
to find the way of peace. That way, however, you cannot
discover if you do not pray. Therefore, dear children, forsake
everything and consecrate your time to God and then God will
bestow gifts upon you and bless you. Little children, do not
forget that your life is fleeting like the spring flower which

today is wondrously beautiful, but tomorrow has vanished. Therefore, pray in such a way that your prayer, your surrender to God may become like a road sign. That way, your witness will not only have value for yourselves, but for all of eternity. Thank you for having responded to my call."

April 25, 1988

"Dear children, God wants to make you holy. Therefore, through me He is calling you to complete surrender. Let the Holy Mass be your life. Understand that the Church is God's palace, the place in which I gather you and want to show you the way to God. Come and pray! Neither look to others nor slander them, but rather let your life be a testimony on the way of holiness. Churches deserve respect and are set apart as holy because God, Who became Man, dwells in them day and night. Therefore, little children, believe and pray that the Father increases your faith, and then ask for whatever you need. I am with you and I rejoice because of your conversion and I am protecting you with my motherly mantle. Thank you for having responded to my call."

May 25, 1988

"Dear children, I am calling you to a complete surrender to God. Pray, little children, that Satan does not sway you like branches in the wind. Be strong in God. I desire that through you the whole world may get to know the God of joy. Neither be anxious nor worried. God will help you and show you the way. I want you to love all men with my love, both the good and the bad. Only that way will love conquer the world. Little children, you are mine. I love you and I want you to surrender to me so I can lead you to God. Pray without ceasing so that Satan cannot take advantage of you. Pray so that you realize that you are mine. I bless you with the blessing of joy. Thank you for having responded to my call."

June 25, 1988

"Dear children, today I am calling you to the love which is
loyal and pleasing to God. Little children, love bears
everything bitter and difficult for the sake of Jesus Who is
love. Therefore, dear children, pray God to come to your aid,
not, however, according to your desires but according to His
love. Surrender yourselves to God so that He may heal you,
console you, and forgive everything inside you which is a
hindrance on the way of love. In this way, God can mold your
life and you will grow in love. Dear children, glorify God with
the canticle of love so that God's love may be able to grow in
you day by day to its fullness. Thank you for having
responded to my call."

July 25, 1988

"Dear children, today I am calling you to a complete surrender
to God. Everything you do and everything you possess give
over to God so that He can take control in your life as King of
all that you possess. That way, through me God can lead you
into the depths of the spiritual life. Little children, do not be
afraid because I am with you even when you think there is no
way out and that Satan is in control. I am bringing peace to
you. I am your Mother and the Queen of Peace. I am blessing
you with the blessing of joy so that for you God may be
everything in life. Thank you for having responded to my call."

August 25, 1988

"Dear children, today I invite you all to rejoice in the life which
God gives you. Little children, rejoice in God the Creator
because He has created you so wonderfully. Pray that your life
be a joyful thanksgiving, which flows out of your heart like a
river of joy. Little children, give thanks unceasingly for all
that you possess, for each little gift, which God has given you
so that a joyful blessing always comes down from God upon
your life. Thank you for having responded to my call."

September 25, 1988

"Dear children, today I am calling all of you without exception
to the way of holiness in your life. God gave you the gift of
holiness. Pray that you may more and more comprehend it
and in that way, you will be able by your life to bear witness
for God. Dear children, I am blessing you and I intercede for
you to God so that your way and your witness may be a
complete one and a joy for God. Thank you for having
responded to my call."

October 25, 1988

"Dear children, my call that you live the messages which I am
giving you is a daily one, especially, little children, because I
want to draw you closer to the Heart of Jesus. Therefore, little
children, I am calling you today to the prayer of Consecration
to Jesus, my dear Son, so that each of your hearts may be His.
And then I am calling you to Consecration to my Immaculate
Heart. I want you to consecrate yourselves as persons,
families, and parishes so that all belongs to God through my
hands. Therefore, dear little children, pray that you may
comprehend the greatness of this message which I am giving
you. I do not want anything for myself, rather, all for the
salvation of your souls. Satan is strong and, therefore, you,
little children, by constant prayer press tightly to my motherly
heart. Thank you for having responded to my call."

The next three Monthly Messages were given while Marija was in
America. See Part II, Chapter 5 - American Messages.

November 25, 1988

"Dear children, I am calling you to prayer so that in prayer
you have an encounter with God. God is offering and giving
Himself to you. But He seeks from you that you answer His
call in your freedom. Therefore, little children, set a time
during the day when you can pray in peace and humility and

meet with God the Creator. I am with you and I intercede with God for you. So be on watch that every encounter in prayer be a joyful meeting with God. Thank you for having responded to my call."

December 25, 1988 (SPECIAL BLESSING)

"Dear children, I am calling you to peace. Live peace in your heart and in your surroundings, so that all may recognize the peace, which does not come from you, but from God. Little children, today is a great day. Rejoice with me! Celebrate the birth of Jesus with my peace, the peace with which I came as your Mother, Queen of Peace. Today I am giving you my Special Blessing. Carry it to every creature so that each one may have peace. Thank you for having responded to my call."

January 25, 1989

"Dear children, today I am calling you to the way of holiness. Pray that you may comprehend the beauty and the greatness of this way, where God reveals Himself to you in a special way. Pray that you may be open to everything that God is doing through you and that in your life you may be enabled to give thanks to God and to rejoice over everything that He is doing through each individual. I am giving you my blessing. Thank you for having responded to my call."

February 25, 1989

"Dear children, today I am calling you to prayer of the heart. Throughout this season of grace, I desire each of you to be united with Jesus; but without unceasing prayer, you cannot experience the beauty and greatness of the grace which God is offering you. Therefore, little children, at all times fill your heart with even the smallest prayers. I am with you and unceasingly I keep watch over every heart which is given to me. Thank you for having responded to my call."

March 25, 1989

"Dear children, I am calling you to a complete surrender to God. I am calling you to great joy and peace which only God can give. I am with you and I intercede for you everyday before God. I call you, little children, to listen to me and to live the messages which I am giving you. For years you have been invited to holiness, but you are still far away. I am blessing you. Thank you for your response to my call."

April 25, 1989

"Dear children, I am calling you to a complete surrender to God. Let everything that you possess be in the hands of God. Only in that way shall you have joy in your heart. Little children, rejoice in everything that you have and give thanks to God because everything is God's gift to you. That way in your life you should be able to give thanks for everything and discover God in everything, even in the smallest flower. Thank you for your response to my call."

May 25, 1989

"Dear children, I am calling you to openness to God. You see, little children, how nature is opening herself and is giving life and fruits. In the same way I am calling you to a life with God and a complete surrender to Him. Little children, I am with you and unceasingly I desire to lead you into the joy of life. I desire that each one of you discovers the joy and the love which is found only in God and which only God can give. God wants nothing else from you but your surrender. Therefore, little children, decide seriously for God because everything passes away. God alone does not pass away. Pray that you may discover the greatness and the joy of life which God is giving you. Thank you for having responded to my call."

June 25, 1989

"Dear children, today I call you to live the messages which I
have been giving you during the past eight years. This is a
time of graces and I desire that the grace of God be great for
every single one of you. I am blessing you and I love you with
a special love. Thank you for having responded to my call."

July 25, 1989

"Dear children, today I am calling you to renew your heart.
Open yourself to God and surrender to Him all your
difficulties and crosses so God may turn everything into joy.
Little children, you cannot open yourselves to God if you do
not pray; therefore, from today decide to consecrate a time and
a day only for an encounter with God in silence. In that way
you will be able, with God, to witness my presence here. Little
children, I do not wish to force you; rather, freely give God
your time, like children of God.   Thank you for having
responded to my call."

August 25, 1989

"Dear Children, today I call you to prayer. By means of
prayer, little children, you will obtain joy and peace. Through
prayer you are richer in the mercy of God. Therefore, little
children, let prayer be the light for each one of you.
Especially, I call you to pray so that all those who are far from
God may be converted. Then our hearts shall be richer
because God will rule in the hearts of all men. Therefore, little
children, pray, pray, pray. Let prayer begin to rule in the
whole world. Thank you for your response to my call!"

September 25, 1989

"Dear children, today I invite you to give thanks to God for all
the gifts you have discovered in the course of your life and
even for the least gift you have received. I give thanks with

you and want all of you to experience the joy of these gifts, and I want God to be everything for each one of you. And then, little children, you can grow continuously on the way of holiness. Thank you for responding to my call."

October 25, 1989

"Dear children, today also I am inviting you to prayer. I am always inviting you, but you are still far away. Therefore, from today, decide seriously to dedicate time to God. I am with you and I wish to teach you to pray with the heart. In prayer with the heart, you shall encounter God. Therefore, dear children, pray, pray, pray. Thank you for having responded to my call."

November 25, 1989

"Dear children, I have been inviting you for years by these messages which I am giving you. Little children, by means of the messages I wish to make a very beautiful mosaic in your heart so I may be able to present each one of you to God like the original image. Therefore, little children, I desire that your decisions be free before God, because He has given you freedom. Therefore, pray so that, free from any influence of Satan, you may decide only for God. I am praying for you before God and I am seeking your surrender to God. Thank you for responding to my call."

December 25, 1989 (SPECIAL BLESSING)

"Dear children, today I bless you in a special way with my Motherly Blessing and I intercede for you to God for Him to give you the gift of the conversion of the heart. For years I have been calling you to encourage you to a profound spiritual life in simplicity, but you are so cold!   Therefore, little children, accept with seriousness and live the messages for your soul not to be sad when I will not be with you anymore and when I will not guide you anymore like an insecure child in his first steps. Therefore, little children, read everyday the

messages I gave you and transform them into life. I love you
and this is why I call you to the way of salvation with God.
Thank you for having responded to my call."

January 25, 1990

"Dear children, today I invite you to decide for God once again
and to choose Him before everything and above everything, so
that He may work miracles in your life and that day by day your
life may become joy with Him. Therefore, little children, pray and
do not permit Satan to work in your life through
misunderstandings, not understanding and not accepting one
another. Pray that you may be able to comprehend the greatness
and the beauty of the gift of life. Thank you for having responded
to my call."

February 25, 1990

"Dear children! I invite you to surrender to God. In this
season I especially want you to renounce all the things to
which you are attached but are hurting your spiritual life.
Therefore, little children, decide completely for God, and do
not allow Satan to come into your life through those things
that hurt both you and your spiritual life. Little children, God
is offering Himself to you in fullness, and you can discover
and recognize Him only in prayer. Therefore, make a decision
for prayer! Thank you for having responded to my call."

March 25, 1990

"Dear children, I am with you even if you are not conscious of
it. I want to protect you from everything that Satan offers you
and through which he wants to destroy you. As I bore Jesus
in my womb, so also, dear children, do I wish to bear you unto
holiness. God wants to save you and sends you messages
through men, nature, and so many things which can only help
you to understand that you must change the direction of your
life. Therefore, little children, understand also the greatness

of the gift which God is giving you through me, so that I may protect you with my mantle and lead you to the joy of life. Thank you for having responded to my call."

April 25, 1990

"Dear children, today I invite you to accept with seriousness and to live the messages which I am giving you. I am with you and I desire, dear children, that each one of you be ever closer to my heart. Therefore, little children, pray and seek the will of God in your everyday life. I desire that each one of you discover the way of holiness and grow in it until eternity. I will pray for you and intercede for you before God that you understand the greatness of this gift which God is giving me that I can be with you. Thank you for having responded to my call."

May 25, 1990

"Dear children, I invite you to decide with seriousness to live this novena [in preparation for Pentecost]. I am with you and I desire to help you to grow in renunciation and mortification that you may be able to understand the beauty of the life of people, who go on giving themselves to me in a special way. Dear children, God blesses you day after day and desires a change of your life. Therefore, pray that you may have the strength to change your life. Thank you for having responded to my call."

June 25, 1990 (SPECIAL BLESSING)

"Dear children, today I desire to thank you for all your sacrifices and for all your prayers. I am blessing you with My Special Motherly Blessing. I invite you all to decide for God and from day to day to discover His will in prayer. I desire, dear children, to call all of you to a full conversion so that joy will be in your hearts. I am happy that you are here today in

such great numbers. Thank you for having responded to my call."

July 25, 1990

"Dear children, today I invite you to peace. I have come here as the Queen of Peace and I desire to enrich you with my motherly peace. Dear children, I love you and I desire to bring all of you to the peace which God gives and which enriches every heart. I invite you to become carriers and witnesses of my peace to this unpeaceful world. Let peace rule in the whole world, which is without peace and longs for peace. I bless you with my motherly blessing. Thank you for having responded to my call."

August 25, 1990

"Today I desire to invite you to take with seriousness and put into practice the messages which I am giving you. You know, little children, that I am with you, that I desire to lead you along the same path to heaven which is beautiful for those who discover it in prayer. Therefore, little children, do not forget that these messages which I am giving you have to be put into your everyday life in order that you might be able to say: 'There, I have taken the messages and tried to live them.' Dear children, I am protecting you before the Heavenly Father by my own prayers. Thank you for having responded to my call."

September 25, 1990

"Dear children, I invite you to prayer with the heart, in order that your prayer may be a conversation with God. I desire each one of you to dedicate more time to God. Satan is strong and wants to destroy and deceive you in many ways. Therefore, my dear children, pray every day that your lives would be a goodness for yourselves and for all those you meet. I am with you and I am protecting you even though Satan

wishes to destroy my plans and hinder the desires which the
Heavenly Father wants to realize here. Thank you for having
responded to my call."

October 25, 1990   .

"Dear children, today I call you to pray in a special way and to
offer up sacrifices and good deeds for peace in the world.
Satan is strong and, with all his strength, tries to destroy the
peace which comes from God. Therefore, dear children, pray
in a special way with me for peace. I am with you and I desire
to help you with my prayers and I desire to guide you on the
path of peace. I bless you with my Motherly Blessing. Do not
forget to live the messages of peace. Thank you for responding
to my call."

November 25, 1990

"Dear children, today I invite you to do works of mercy with
love and out of love for me and for your and my brothers and
sisters. All that you do for others, do it with great joy and
humility towards God. I am with you and day after day I offer
your sacrifices and prayers to God for the salvation of the
world. Thank you for having responded to my call!"

December 25, 1990

"Dear children, today I invite you in a special way to pray for
peace. Dear children, without peace you cannot experience the
birth of the little Jesus neither today nor in your daily lives.
Therefore, pray the Lord of peace that He may protect you
with His mantle and that He may help you to comprehend the
greatness and the importance of peace in your hearts. In this
way, you shall be able to spread peace from your hearts
throughout the whole world. I am with you and I intercede for
you before God. Pray because Satan wants to destroy my
plans of peace. Be reconciled with one another and by means

of your lives help peace to reign on the whole earth. Thank
you for having responded to my call.

January 25, 1991

"Dear children, today, like never before, I invite you to prayer.
Your prayer should be a prayer for peace. Satan is strong and
wishes not only to destroy human life but also nature and the
planet on which you live. Therefore, dear children, pray that
you can protect yourselves through prayer with the blessing of
God's peace. God sent me to you so that I can help you. If
you wish to, grasp for the Rosary. Already, the Rosary alone
can do miracles in the world and in your lives. I bless you
and I stay among you as long as it is God's will. Thank you
that you will not betray my presence here and I thank you
because your response is serving God and peace. Thank you
for having responded to my call!

February 25, 1990

"Dear children, today I invite you to decide for God because
distance from God is the fruit of the lack of peace in your
hearts. God is peace itself. Therefore, approach Him through
your personal prayer and then live peace in your hearts, and
in this way peace will flow from your hearts like a river into
the whole world. Do not speak about peace, but make peace.
I am blessing each of you and each good decision of yours.
Thank you for having responded to my call.

March 25, 1991

"Again today I invite you to live the passion of Jesus in prayer,
and in union with Him. Decide to give more time to God who
gave you these days of grace. Therefore, dear children, pray
and renew in a special way the love for Jesus in your hearts.
I am with you and I accompany you with my blessing and my
prayers. Thank you for having responded to my call."

April 25, 1991

"Dear children, today I invite you all so that your prayer be prayer with the heart. Let each of you find time for prayer, so that in your prayer you discover God. I do not desire you to talk about prayer, but to pray. Let your every day be filled with prayer of gratitude to God for life and for all that you have. I do not desire your life to pass by in words, but that you glorify God with deeds. I am with you and I am grateful to God for every moment spent with you. Thank you for having responded to my call!"

May 25, 1991

"Dear children, today I invite all of you who have heard my message of peace to realize it with seriousness and with love in your life. There are many who think that they are doing a lot by talking about the messages but do not live them. Dear children, I invite you to life and to change all the negative in you, so that it all turns into the positive and life. Dear children, I am with you and I desire to help each of you to live and, by living, to witness the good news. I am here, dear children, to help you and to lead you to heaven, and in heaven is the joy through which you can already live heaven now. Thank you for having responded to my call!"

The indexes do not include the following message.

June 25, 1991 (TENTH ANNIVERSAY)

This Tenth Anniversary message has a lot more to it than appears here. It should be read with prayer.

"Dear children, today on this great day which you have given to me, I desire to bless all of you and to say: These days while I am with you are days of grace. I desire to teach you and to help you walk on the path of holiness. There are many people who do not desire to understand my messages and to accept with seriousness what I am saying. But you I therefore call and ask that by your lives and your daily living you witness my presence. If you pray, God will help you discover the true reason for my coming. Therefore, little children, pray and read the Sacred Scriptures so that through my coming you discover the message in Sacred Scripture for you. Thank you for responding to my call."

CHAPTER 4

THE MESSAGES
OF OUR LADY
TO THE PRAYER GROUP

(January 25, 1988 to July 5, 1991)

Marija, Ivan, and others formed a Prayer Group. This group assembles on Monday nights on Apparition Mountain around 9:00 p.m. They pray and sing and Our Lady usually appears to the two visionaries about 10:30 p.m.; She sometimes gives a message. On Friday nights this group sometimes goes to Cross Mountain. During these meetings with Our Lady, there have been up to tens of thousands of people present on some occasions.

Our Lady always says, **"Praised be Jesus,"** when she comes and, after giving Her message, prays The Lord's Prayer and one Glory Be with the group. She leaves in the sign of the light of the cross saying, **"Go in the peace of God."**

January 25, 1988

"Thank you for this evening, you have helped me very much. Continue to pray for my intentions."

February 1, 1988

"Prepare yourself for the time of Lent by renouncing something. During Lent I will need your help for the accomplishment and fulfillment of all my plans."

February 8, 1988

"I'm asking you, yourself, to decide for the way of Holiness. Dear children, I want to help you.

She went back to the sky joyfully as always.

February 15, 1988

"Be the reflection of Jesus. This way, you will be His witnesses in your lives; but you cannot be His reflection without prayer."

February 22, 1988

"Thank you for the things you have renounced during Lent. Most of all, renounce sin. Be light, to shine for others. Encourage others to prayer, fasting, and penance. Give love to others."

February 29, 1988

"Dear children, give all problems and difficulties to Jesus and pray. Pray, pray, pray! Every evening during this month, pray in front of the Crucifix in thanksgiving until the death of Jesus."

March 7, 1988

"I am your Mother and I want to warn you that Satan wants to destroy everything we have started, so pray a lot."

March 14, 1988

"Dear children, in this period of Lent Satan is trying by every means to destroy in you what we have started. I warn you as a Mother, let prayer be your weapon against him."

March 21, 1988

"Dear children, today again your Mother wants to warn you that Satan, by every means possible, wants to ruin everything in you; but your prayers prevent him from succeeding. When you fill up all the empty spaces with prayer, you prevent Satan from entering your soul. Pray, dear children, and your Mother will pray with you to defeat Satan. May this time be the time in which all of us give and distribute peace to others. Therefore, please spread peace in your homes, in your families, in the streets, and everywhere."

March 28, 1988

"Pray as much as you can before Easter. Everyday pray two hours before the Crucifix."

April 4, 1988

"Give love and joy to others and pray for peace."

April 11, 1988

"Dear children, I am your Mother and I am asking you to convert. Pray now for people who curse against the Name of God."

April 18, 1988

No apparition.

May 9, 1988

"May this month be for you the month of the Rosary and reading your bible. Satan wants to disturb your plans."

May 21, 1988

Our Lady came joyfully. She prayed The Lord's Prayer and one Glory Be with the visionary as She always does.

June 6, 1988

"Dear children, it's going to be seven years soon that I have been coming to you. I ask you to renew in yourselves the messages I have given to you. These are messages of prayer, peace, fasting, and penance. Make some penance yourselves. All of the other messages come from these four basic ones, but also live the other ones. Thank you for responding to my call. I am your Mother. Open your heart to the grace."

June 13, 1988

Our Lady repeated Monday's message (June 6, 1988).

June 23, 1988

"Dear children, I am happy and so is my Son. Go to confession to have a pure heart for the anniversary. Come to pray on the hill tomorrow between ten and midnight, but I will not appear."

June 27, 1988

"Dear children, your Mother loves you all. I'm happy to see you here, dear children. I give you love; give this love to others. Be peace workers. Help the others to change their lives. I give you might, dear children; with this might, you can bear everything. May this might make you strong in everything. You need it; that is why I give you might."

July 4, 1988

"Dear children, I am your Mother and I warn you this time is a time of temptation. Satan is trying to find emptiness in you, so he can enter and destroy you. DO NOT SURRENDER! I pray with you. Do not pray just with your lips, but pray with the heart. In this way prayer will obtain victory!

August 1, 1988

"I ask you to pray a lot these days before Friday. I would like you to live this Friday in joy. I also ask you tonight, when you go to your houses, to pray the Glorious Mysteries in front of the crucifix."

August 4, 1988

"My dear children, tonight my Son has sent me among you. I am happy with you. I am happy to see you in such a large number. I would like your joy to remain this whole day. Live this joy in prayer, live in joy. I give you love so you can live with love. Extend love around you. Your Mother loves you. I am happy tonight. I want your cooperation. I want to work with you. Your cooperation is necessary to me. I cannot do anything without you."

August 8, 1988

"Dear children, your Mother asks you to pray for all the young people in the world. Renew yourselves in prayer before the feast day."

August 12, 1988

"Dear children, your Mother asks you to pray as much as you can during these two days. Prepare yourselves in prayer for the feast to come. Dear children, I would like to tell you to bring peace to others during these days. Encourage others to change.   You cannot, dear children, give peace if you, yourselves, are not at inner peace. Tonight I give you peace. Give peace to others! **Dear children, be a light that shines. I ask you pray the Glorious Mysteries when you go back to your homes tonight. Pray them in front of the crucifix."**

August 15, 1988 (SPECIAL BLESSING)
(FEAST OF THE ASSUMPTION and the end of the Marian Year)

"Dear children, from today on I would like you to start a New Year, the Year of the Young People. During this year pray for the young people; talk with them.   Young people find themselves now in a very difficult situation. Help each other. I think about you in a special way, dear children.   Young people have a role to play in the Church now. Pray, dear children."

August 19, 1988

"Dear children, I would like this time to be the time of decision. Make a decision, dear children, follow me, follow me! I cannot do anything, and I want to do a lot, but I cannot do it without you. Your decisions are weak! Pray, dear children, during this time. Only through prayer can you receive this strength, this vigor. I will help you, dear children."

August 22, 1988

"My dear children, with your prayers you have helped me to fulfill the plan. Praised be Jesus, my dear children. Dear children, I would like to tell you tonight, during these days especially pray for the young. I would like to recommend to "my" priests to create and organize groups where young people are taught and given good advice for their lives. You, dear children, who are present tonight, you, must be the messengers of the good word of peace to others, to young people especially. Your Mother wants to pray for you all tonight."

August 29, 1988

"Dear children, thank God, the Creator, even for little things. I would like you to thank God for your family, for the place where you work, and for the people God puts in your way."

September 5, 1988

"My dear children, tonight your Mother warns you that in this time Satan desires you and is looking for you! A little spiritual emptiness in you is enough for Satan to work in you. For this reason your Mother invites you to begin to pray. May your weapon be prayer. With prayer with the heart you will overcome Satan. Your Mother invites you to pray for the young people in the whole world."

September 9, 1988

"Dear children, tonight also your Mother is warning that Satan is at work. I would like you to pay special attention to the fact that Satan is at work in a special way with the young. Dear children, during this period I would like you to pray in your families with your children. I would like you to talk with your children. I would like you to exchange your experiences and help them to solve all their problems. I will pray, dear children, for the young, for all of you. Pray, dear children. Prayer is medicine that heals."

September 12, 1988

The message for tonight's encounter is:

Our Lady calls us all to pray during this time for the hungry and poor people in the whole world. She thanks us in a special way tonight because we helped Her to fulfill the plan.

October 17, 1988

"Dear children, tonight your Mother is happy, joyful together with you. I would like to extend happiness to you. I would like to give you love, so you can bring this love and spread it to others. I would like to give you peace, so you can give this peace to others, so you can give this peace especially to families where hatred exists. I would like you, dear children, to renew the family prayer, all of you. I would like you to encourage others to renew this prayer. Your Mother will help you."

October 24, 1988

"Dear children, your Mother wants to call you to pray for the young of the whole world, for the parents of the whole world so they know how to educate their children and how to lead them in life with good advice. Pray, dear children; the situation of the young is difficult. Help them! Help parents who don't know, who give bad advice!"

October 31, 1988

"Dear children, tonight your mother wants to encourage you to begin to pray with the heart. This prayer is necessary to today's human being for today's world. Do not pray just with your lips. Do not pray if you don't know what you pray. During this period too, dear children, I need your prayers, because I have great plans. I want to collaborate with you. I have repeated that many times in my messages. I need you. Because of that, pray, pray with the heart!"

November 7, 1988

"Dear children, this is a time for grace. That is why I would like you to pray as much as you can during this time. Especially, I would like you to renew the family prayer!"

November 11, 1988 (SPECIAL BLESSING)

Our Lady appeared with five angels and gave a Special Blessing during the 30-minute apparition to Vicka.

"Dear children, you know this time is a time of special graces; that is why I ask you to renew in you the messages that I give. Live those messages with the heart."

November 14, 1988 - To Vicka:

"Dear children, I bless you with my Motherly Blessing, and I ask you to be the carriers of my peace and to pray for peace in the world."

December 24, 1988

"My dear children, these are days of joy. Give me all your problems and live in joy."

January 2, 1989

"My dear children, for this year I want to tell you, pray! Your Mother loves you. I want to collaborate with you for I need your collaboration. I want you to become, dear children, my announcers and my sons who will bring peace, love, conversion .... I want you to be a sign for others. In this new year I want to give you peace; I want to give you love and harmony. Abandon all your problems and all your difficulties to me. Live my messages. Pray, pray!"

January 9, 1989

"Dear children, pray because Satan is very active in this time. He wants to destroy everything you have received from me. During these days I invite you to renew the prayer in your families and to pray all the Mysteries of the Rosary every evening."

February 6, 1989 (SPECIAL BLESSING)

Ivan says: "Our Lady wants this from us during Lent.

1. Review and live Her messages.
2. Read the Bible more.
3. Pray more and offer all for the intentions of Our Lady.
4. Make more sacrifices.

Our Lady will be with us and will accompany us. She gave a 'SPECIAL BLESSING.'"

February 13, 1989

> "Dear children, remember the four things you have to do during Lent. Tonight when you go home, I ask you to be thankful in front of the crucifix for all that you feel you should be grateful for; thank Jesus for what you want. My Son will hear you."

February 17, 1989

> "Dear children, tonight I don't ask you to do anything special. I only wish you to begin to live my messages. Dear children, I seek your action, not your words! You are all happy when I give you a beautiful message, but live the message I give! May each message be for you a new growth. Take this message into your life, in this way you will grow in life. Your Mother cannot give you other messages if you don't live the ones I already gave you. Begin tonight to live the messages."

February 24, 1989

> "Tonight when you go home, pray The Lord's Prayer, the Hail Mary, and the Glory Be seven times; and then pray The Lord Prayer, the Hail Mary, and the Glory Be five times."

February 27, 1989

"Dear children, during this time multiply your prayers and go deeper into the messages that I have given. Tonight when you go home, pray the Joyful Mysteries in front of the crucifix."

March 3, 1989

"Dear children, I thank you because by your coming here you have helped to fulfill the plan of God. During this time pray and renew yourselves. Tonight when you come home, pray the Joyful Mysteries in front of the crucifix.

March 17, 1989

"I ask you again to multiply your prayers to prepare yourself for Easter. Also, read the Bible, especially those passages that tell about the Passion of Jesus. Prepare yourself to look at Jesus 'eye to eye.' Tonight when you come home, pray in front of the crucifix in thanksgiving for all the graces you receive."

March 20, 1989

"Tonight I ask you to begin from today to pray all the more. Contemplate the wounds of Jesus. Pray as much as you can in front of the crucifix. May the cross be (just) for you in the day (of the cross.)"

March 24, 1989 (GOOD FRIDAY)

"Dear children, tonight your Mother is happy to see you in such large numbers. I wish, dear children, that you start from today to live a different life. Your Mother gives you love; give this love to others so we can be ready to live Easter. When you go back in your homes finish this day in prayer."

March 27, 1989 (EASTER MONDAY)

"Dear children, your Mother calls you to completely surrender to God. Dear children, this is a time of grace. Pray as much as you can and renew yourself through prayer. Construct yourself spiritually. This construction lasts until the end of your life. Continue to pray as much as you can and with your prayers you will help me."

May 5, 1989

"Dear children, tonight your mother invites you to pray as much as you can during this time. This is a time of grace. Abandon yourselves to the Spirit for Him to renew you. May prayer renew your bodies, your souls, your hearts. Don't let your bodies be weak. You know that the Spirit is always willing."

May 12, 1989

"Now is a time of special graces, but Satan is very active."

June 6, 1989

"Dear children, the Mother is happy to be with all of you. Dear children, you have helped me to realize the plans of God. I want to speak to you about love and give you love. In these days, prepare yourselves for the anniversary of the apparitions with love, with my messages, and with joy and the Mother will help you, dear children, and the Mother will stay with you. There is nothing more important for you but to put what I have said in first place."

June 16, 1989

"Dear children, I want more penance from you."

June 23, 1989

"Dear children, I am happy to see you in such a large number. I would like to pray for you in a special way tonight. Dear children, give me the day that comes (June 24, 1989) in prayer."

June 26, 1989

"Dear children, your Mother told you yesterday to renew the messages from now on. Your Mother asks, especially from you of the group of prayer, to live from now on the messages in prayer. If you want your Mother to give other and new messages, you first have to live those messages I have already given."

July 3, 1989

"Dear children, your Mother asks you tonight, you, who are present (people were present from all over the world), when you get back into your home, renew prayer in your family. Take time for prayer, dear children. I, as your Mother, especially want to tell you that the family has to pray together. The Holy Spirit wants to be present in the families. Allow the Holy Spirit to come. The Holy Spirit comes through prayer. That is why, pray and allow the Holy Spirit to renew you, to renew today's family. Your Mother will help you."

July 10, 1989

"Dear children, you know we are living the Year of the Young People. This year ends on August 15. Your Mother wishes to dedicate one more year to the youth. Not only to the youth, may this year also be the year of the family. Dear children, in these days before the fifteenth of August, prepare yourselves, you and your family, for the new year to come so it may be the Year of the Family."

July 14, 1989

"Dear children, you know that we live the year of the young
people. This year ends on August 15. Your Mother wishes to
dedicate one more year to the youth, but not only to the youth.
May this year also be the year of the family. Dear children,
in these days before the fifteenth of August, prepare yourselves,
you and your family, for the new year to come, so it may be the
year of the family."

July 17, 1989

"Dear children, I would like to call you to start again to live
the messages. More than eight years ago your Mother told
four messages: Peace, Conversion, Sacrifice, and Faith. Dear
children, I would like you to live the messages through prayer.
I know how much you give me promises through words, but,
dear children, I want you to put that into practice. I will pray,
dear children, and I will help you. Conversion is a process
which goes on through your entire life."

July 21, 1989

"Pray for my intentions."

July 24, 1989

"Dear children, tonight your Mother is happy to see you in
such large numbers. Your Mother wants to give you love
tonight so you can give and share this love with others when
you will come back to your homes. Live love. I want to give
you peace, so you can carry it to others. You cannot give peace
to others if you don't have this peace within yourselves. I need
you, dear children, to cooperate with me, because there are
today many plans that I cannot fulfill without you. I need
your cooperation. Pray, pray, pray."

July 31, 1989

"Dear children, tonight especially I would like to invite all the
parents in the world to find time for their children and family.
May they offer love to their children. May this love that they
offer be parental and motherly love. Once again, dear
children, I call you to family prayer. During one of the
previous encounters your Mother asked you to renew the
family prayer. I ask that again tonight. During this period,
let us pray together for all the young people in the world."

August 7, 1989

"Tonight your Mother wants to call you to prayer. This is a
time of grace. Pray, dear children, and your Mother will pray
together with you. Abandon to your Mother all your problems
and difficulties."

August 11, 1989

"I call you to prayer, like I have done also in the previous
encounter. I ask that during the three days to come each one
of you make a sacrifice, give up something that is dear to you
in life. Give up something especially during those three days."

August 14, 1989 - SPECIAL BLESSING

"My dear children, tonight your Mother is happy, happy,
happy to be with you and to see you in such large numbers.
I am happy for what we have done in this Year of the Youth.
We have stepped a step forward. I would like to see in the
future parents in the families work and pray as much as they
can with their children, so they can, from day to day,
strengthen their spirit. Your Mother is here to help each one
of you; open yourselves to your Mother; She is waiting for you.
May this moment you will live at midnight be a moment of
thanksgiving for everything you received during this year."

August 18, 1989

"**Dear children, tonight your Mother asks you in this period of time to pray for peace in the world.**"

August 21, 1989

"**Tonight your Mother wants to invite you to start again to live the messages. Children, your Mother cannot give you new messages if you do not live the messages I have already given. Decide with love and joy to begin to live the messages, for your Mother to continue to guide you, for you to continue your growth in love with your Mother living the messages.**"

December 15, 1989

"**Prepare yourselves spiritually and physically for the Christmas Novena. In your prayers say one prayer especially for my intentions. Renounce [give up] something that you like the most.**"

December 18, 1989

"**The prayers and sacrifices that you decide to offer in these days when I asked you were not done with love. I ask you to offer them with love as during the first days of the Apparitions. What you have decided to do and to offer for my intentions during the novena was not enough. You have to choose to give more because you are able.**"

Our Lady prayed [in Hebrew] in Her Mother tongue.

December 21, 1989

From Marija to Father Luciano:

"Our Lady asked me to pray and offer sacrifices for priests."

December 22, 1989

Marija:

"Our Lady says this Christmas should be the most beautiful Christmas of your life."

December 22, 1989

"Dear children, tonight your Mother wants to call you to prayer, call you to prayer during those two days. Through prayer open your hearts and let us wait all together for this day which is for us the day of joy. Dear children, I wish you to decide to do something concrete during these two days."

December 25, 1989

"Dear children, here is my Son in my arms! I would like to ask you to be a light for all in the year to come. I would like to call you again to live the messages, those are messages of peace, conversion, prayer, penance, and faith. Dear children, your Mother does not ask words from you, I ask for deeds. Your Mother will help you and She will give you the strength to continue. And tonight I would like to tell you: Rejoice!"

January 1, 1990

"Dear children, tonight your Mother would like to call you, like I have done before, to renew prayer in the families. Dear children, the family needs to pray today. I wish, dear children, that you would renew [start again to live] my messages through this prayer."

February 2, 1990

"Pray for peace, everybody present - not just the group - pray for peace."

February 5, 1990

"Pray for peace, especially you from the group, pray for peace."

February 9, 1990

"Our Lady asks that prayer meetings would last two hours, an hour of singing, an hour of prayer."

Only this part of the message was told by Ivan, the rest is secret, just for the group.

February 12, 1990

"Dear children, your Mother is happy when She sees you in such large numbers. Dear children, you have come to me with a firm decision. Do not fear anything, I protect you and guard you. I wish, dear children, tonight again to call you to prayer because I need your help for the fulfillment of my plans. I need your cooperation [participation], dear children. Thank you for having responded to my call."

February 19, 1990

"Dear children, your Mother tonight wants to warn you that Satan is active in a special way these days. Don't allow emptiness inside of you, fill this emptiness with prayer. Dear children, these days prayer is the best medicine to defend yourselves against evil. In a special way, dear children, make a decision through prayer for Lent. Tonight I am expecting from you to pray the Glorious Mysteries when you return home."

March 2, 1990

"Dear children, tonight your Mother asks and pleads: Abandon to me all your problems, all your hardships. I want to prepare you for the day that comes free from all your problems. Give me all your problems."

March 5, 1990

"Do something concrete for Easter."

March 23, 1990

"Dear children, tonight again your Mother wants to call you to prayer. Dear children, I need your prayer to fulfill the plans I have now with you and in the world also. Thank you, dear children, for listening to me. Dear children, thank you for having responded to my call."

April 13, 1990 - GOOD FRIDAY

"Dear children, I am happy to see you tonight. You know, dear children, that when my Son was dying I was alone with Him with just some other women, and so I am happy to see you here tonight in such large numbers. Tonight also when you go back home, pray a Rosary in front of the crucifix and be thankful [to God]."

May 7, 1990

"Dear children, your Mother is so happy tonight to see you all. I want tonight to call you again to pray the rosary, and to pray this month especially, because I am in need of your prayers."

May 11, 1990

"Dear children, tonight your Mother is happy to see you. Tonight especially, I want to ask you to give me your problems and difficulties so that you are able to pray with more freedom and more joy so that your prayer becomes a prayer with the heart. That is why I wish to ask you tonight to release yourselves from your difficulties through prayer; and I will pray for you. Dear children, I need your prayers."

May 21, 1990

"Dear children, tonight your Mother invites you to pray for Peace. I need your prayers for peace these days, dear children. Pray, pray, pray."

May 25, 1990

"Dear children, tonight again your Mother wants to call you to prayer. Especially live, accept, and accomplish in prayer the message I gave tonight [May 25 Monthly Message]. I need your prayers, dear children. This is why: pray, pray, pray!"

June 1, 1990

"Dear children, this is a time of grace. Open yourselves to the Holy Spirit, for the Holy Spirit to make you strong. Your Mother, dear children, wants especially to call you in this time to prayer and to sacrifice."

June 8, 1990

"Dear children, your Mother is happy tonight to see you in such large numbers. Tonight also your Mother calls you to prayer. Dear children, prayer is necessary for me to fulfill many plans that I wish to accomplish. Especially tonight, I invite you to pray the Glorious Mysteries of the Rosary in front of the crucifix when you go back to your homes. Pray these mysteries for my intentions."

June 22, 1990

"Dear children, I am happy to see you in such large numbers. Tonight again your Mother asks you to prepare yourselves through prayers during these two days for the day that comes."

June 25, 1990

"Dear children, your Mother invites you to joy. Your Mother asks you to begin to live tonight's message [the monthly message given earlier to Marija]. Your Mother, again tonight, asks you to give me all your problems and all your hardships. Thank you, dear children, because we are going to continue to live in prayer everything that I say."

July 13, 1990

"Dear children, your Mother asks you, especially in this period, to pray all the more. Satan wants, in this time, to be active through your weakness. This is why, dear children, your Mother invites you: pray, pray, pray. Do not allow Satan to enter. Close all the entrances. Prayer is the best weapon."

July 23, 1990

"Dear children, tonight your Mother wants especially to invite you to pray in these days for peace."

July 30, 1990

"Dear children, tonight again your Mother would like to invite you in a special way to prayer. Especially you, the youngest, who will be present in large numbers during these days. I invite you to prayer. Pray, pray, pray and renew your hearts to be able to accept later everything I will tell you, all my messages. Thank you, dear children, because you will make me happy by your prayers."

August 3, 1990

"Dear children, tonight again your Mother wants to encourage you to pray all the more during this time. Join together in prayer with the young people. Especially, dear children, your Mother wants you to renew prayer in today's family."

August 10, 1990

"Dear children, your mother tonight wants to call you in a special way to pray for peace."

August 13, 1990

"Dear children, tonight again your mother asks in a special way for you to pray for peace, especially in this time. Pray, dear children, to help your mother to fulfill all that She plans."

August 17, 1990

"Dear children, tonight I ask you to pray for peace in a very special way."

August 20, 1990

"I ask you to pray for peace."

The messages of August 20 and 24 were given to Ivan during his prayer group meeting. Then Our Lady prayed for peace in a different but very special way in front of Ivan.

August 24, 1990

"Pray for peace in a special way."

October 1, 1990

"Dear children, tonight your mother asks you to pray especially for peace in this time."

October 5, 1990

"Pray for peace in this time."

For the first time during the apparitions, Ivan was heard praying The Lord's Prayer and the Glory Be three times with Our Lady. The Gospa told Ivan this prayer was for the intention of peace.

October 10, 1990

"I come here as the Queen of Peace and Reconciliation. I need your prayers and sacrifices especially in this time. Pray for peace in the world."

October 15, 1990

"Dear children, tonight I invite you to pray for peace. Dear children, I want to give you new messages. I am your mother. I always want to teach you something new, but for this you must first live the messages that I have already given you so I can give you new messages."

October 19, 1990

"Pray for peace."

November 16, 1990

To Marija:

"Dear children, I thank you for you have come up here tonight to pray. Your Mother asks you to pray for peace in the world in this time. For that, I ask you to come up often and pray on the Apparition Hill, (Podbrdo), and Krizevac, in order to pray for peace. I also ask you to gather your family to pray together for peace and for the salvation of the world."

This was a very intense apparition. Afterwards, Marija said, "I felt as if Our Lady wanted to take my soul."

November 26, 1990

This message was given to Marija during the prayer group meetin;
on the mountain. Our Lady said She was very happy that the peopl<
had come to pray with Her.

**"Dear children, I desire you to witness my presence through
love."**

December 21, 1990

**"Dear children, tonight your Mother invites you to take this
time to prepare your hearts in prayer for the day that comes,
for Christmas."**

December 24, 1990

Our Lady appeared with three angels.

**"Dear children, tonight your Mother invites you to give Her all
your problems. My dear children, REJOICE!"**

December 31, 1990

**"Dear children, tonight your Mother invites you to go together
with me to the church in joy and in prayer. In this very
specific joy, pray in church for the intention of peace."**

There was a New Year's Eve Mass at 11:30 p.m.

January 7, 1991

At 10:00 p.m. Our Lady came with three angels and prayed for a very
long time with Ivan for peace.

**"Dear children, tonight your Mother calls you in a special way
to pray for peace."**

January 11, 1991

Our Lady appeared to Ivan during his prayer group meeting. Although She did not give a message, She prayed with Ivan for peace. The people who were on the mountain for the prayer meeting felt this action was a strong message from Our Lady, showing that everyone should be praying for peace as She is.

January 14, 1991

The apparition was at 9:30 (Podbrdo). Ivan said that Our Lady prayed for peace with him and thanked the people for coming up the mountain to pray. There was no message. Ivan asked that prayer for peace continue through the night and there was Adoration the whole night in the Chapel in union with 1,000 prayer groups in America. Ivan was present.

March 22, 1991

"Tonight your Mother invites you to pray more. Pray specially in your families, and by prayer prepare for the day that comes, for Easter."

March 29, 1991 (GOOD FRIDAY)

"Dear children, I want to call (invite) you, under this cross, to take your cross as the will of God. As my Son took His cross, so you carry everything, and my Son will be glorified through your crosses. Thank you, dear children, for answering my call and carrying your cross."

April 5, 1991

"Dear children, tonight your mother wants to invite you, especially in this time, to pray together with me for peace."

Then Ivan prayed the Lord's Prayer and Glory Be three times with Our Lady for the intention of peace.

April 8, 1991

"I ask you to pray with me for peace."

May 3, 1991

"Dear children, today your mother wants you to pray in a special way for peace these days. Pray, Pray, Pray. Your prayers are necessary for me."

May 10, 1991

"I invite you to pray for peace!"

May 27, 1991

"I invite you to accept and live the message I gave you on the twenty-fifth."

The following messages are not included in the indexes.

June 17, 1991

"I invite you to pray for peace and for conversion."

July 5, 1991

"Dear children, your Mother wants you to pray for peace in a special way with me in this time."

NOTES AND FUTURE EXPANSION
OF OUR LADY'S MESSAGES

NOTES AND FUTURE EXPANSION
OF OUR LADY'S MESSAGES

NOTES AND FUTURE EXPANSION
OF OUR LADY'S MESSAGES

NOTES AND FUTURE EXPANSION
OF OUR LADY'S MESSAGES

NOTES AND FUTURE EXPANSION
OF OUR LADY'S MESSAGES

NOTES AND FUTURE EXPANSION
OF OUR LADY'S MESSAGES

CHAPTER 5

THE MESSAGES
OF OUR LADY
WHILE MARIJA WAS IN AMERICA

(November 19, 1988 to January 26, 1989)

"I AM HERE TO HELP YOU!" (**November 24, 1988** Thanksgiving Day)

Marija, her brother, and two friends traveled to America where Marija underwent surgery to donate one of her kidneys to her brother, Andreja. They arrived on November 18. Our Lady did many beautiful things. (For more information, see the October 6, 1986 message on Pages 146 - 147 in the section on the Early Messages and Various Other Messages.)

November 19, 1988, 10:40 a.m.

Our Lady came and was very happy. She blessed everyone. Marija recommended everyone present to Our Lady and Our Lady prayed The Lord's Prayer and one Glory Be. Our Lady said She would appear at 10:30 p.m., Sunday night.

November 20, 1988, 10:30 p.m.

Our Lady came and was very happy. She blessed individually everyone in the room. Marija recommended all present to Our Lady and She prayed The Lord's Prayer and the Glory Be. Our Lady's message:

"May your life be prayer. May your work be offered as a prayer and may everything that you do bring you toward me. Let everything that you do and everybody that you meet be an encounter with God."

She made the Sign of the Cross over everyone and left saying, **"Go in peace."**

November 21, 1988, 10:40 a.m. (SPECIAL BLESSING)

Our Lady appeared with three angels and was very happy. She looked around at everybody, even the people outside. A Catholic school closed today so that children could come to the apparition and many were present. Our Lady prayed in Hebrew over the whole crowd. She gave all a SPECIAL BLESSING. Our Lady said,

"Live the messages that I give."

November 22, 1988, 10:40 a.m.

Our Lady came and was very happy. She looked around the crowd of about 400 people, inside and outside the home where Marija was staying. Our Lady blessed everyone. Marija recommended everyone present to Our Lady and She prayed The Lord's Prayer and the Glory Be. Our Lady's message:

"Live in humility all the messages that I give. I want you to be carriers of peace."

Our Lady gave a blessing of peace and left.

November 23, 1988, 10:30 p.m.

Our Lady came and was very happy. She blessed everyone. Marija recommended everyone present to Our Lady and She prayed The Lord's Prayer and the Glory Be. Our Lady's message:

"I invite you to pray and give your life completely to God. I
will give you strength and I will help you in all of your needs.
You can ask for everything that you need to help you. I will
intercede for you in front of God."

The Blessed Mother said She would appear the next morning in a
field near a large pine tree and Our Lady extended an invitation for
all to come.

November 24, 1988, 10:40 a.m.
(THANKSGIVING DAY)

The apparition took place near a large tree in a field near the home
where Marija was staying. Our Lady came and was very happy. She
looked at all who had gathered there. She blessed everyone. Marija
recommended every person present to Our Lady and She prayed The
Lord's Prayer and the Glory Be. Our Lady's message:

"I invite you to live my messages. I am here to help you! I will
intercede for you to God for all your intentions."

Several hundred people were present. When She left, Our Lady said:
"Go in peace."

November 25, 1988, 10:40 a.m.

The next three monthly messages for the world were given to Marija
while she was in Birmingham.

"Dear children, I call you to prayer for you to have an
encounter with God in prayer. God gives Himself to you, but
He wants you to answer in your own freedom to His invitation.
That is why, little children, during the day find yourselves a
special time when you can pray in peace and humility and
have this meeting with God, the Creator. I am with you and
I intercede for you in front of God. Watch in vigil so that
every encounter in prayer be the joy of your contact with God.
Thank you for having responded to my call."

November 26, 1988, 10:40 a.m.

Our Lady came and was very happy. With Her hands extended, She prayed over everyone and blessed them. Marija recommended all those present, especially the sick, to Our Lady and She prayed The Lord's Prayer and the Glory Be. Our Lady's message:

"I ask you once again to pray. Especially pray for my intentions. If you pray for my intentions, I will be glorified through you. All your prayers are going to help you through my hands."

November 27, 1988, 10:30 p.m.

Our Lady came and was very happy. She blessed the people and all their religious objects with the Sign of the Cross. Marija recommended everyone present, especially the sick, to Our Lady and She prayed The Lord's Prayer and the Glory Be. Our Lady's message:

"I want you to be in prayer. I want to protect you under my mantle. Pray. Pray. Pray."

November 28, 1988, 10:30 p.m.

Our Lady came and was very happy. She prayed over everybody. Marija recommended every person present to Our Lady and She prayed The Lord's Prayer and the Glory Be. Our Lady blessed everyone and went to Heaven. No special message.

November 29, 1988, 10:30 p.m. (SPECIAL BLESSING)

Our Lady came and was very happy. She blessed and prayed over everyone. Marija recommended all those present, especially the sick, to Our Lady. Our Lady prayed The Lord's Prayer and the Glory Be. Our Lady extended Her arms above all who gathered there and for a certain time prayed in that manner. Tonight Our Lady gave the SPECIAL BLESSING. Our Lady's message:

"Bless [with the Special Blessing] even those who don't believe. You can give them this Blessing from the heart to help them in their conversion. Bless everyone you meet. I give you a special grace. I desire you to give this grace to others."

Our Lady left saying, **"Go in peace."**

The November 29 SPECIAL BLESSING was given on a day which was not a feast day or a special occasion. Our Lady spoke specifically about what She desired with this SPECIAL BLESSING. This was rare and it was interpreted as Our Lady's desire to spread this important gift. Those gathered in the field were surprised and elated because no one expected this gift.

Marija has said:

1. This is a blessing which has the power to convert and to help people.

2. It may be used on believers and non-believers to help them convert or to progress in their conversion process.

3. Once Our Lady gives it to you, it lasts your whole life.

4. You do not have to be in the presence of the one you are blessing.

5. The blessing is as powerful as the degree of faith you have in it and the prayer you offer. The more you pray from the heart, the stronger it is.

6. If you receive this blessing from Our Lady and in turn bless another with it, that person has it to the same degree you first received it from Our Lady. This second person may then give it to a third, and the third to a fourth, etc. All will receive this gift to bless others just as if Our Lady gave it directly. This blessing will last your entire lifetime.

7. You must be at the site of the apparition to receive it directly from Our Lady.

8. To bless someone, a spontaneous prayer is fine. You can say, "I extend to you the blessing of Our Lady." If you choose to say more, it is acceptable. When giving this Special Blessing to a non-believer, you may do so silently, in his presence or from a distance. You may extend this blessing everyday to help this person to convert.

N.B. The blessing from a priest is Christ's blessing. This Special Blessing is Our Lady's blessing. You should not think of yourself as a priest, blessing as a priest does. Use this blessing in a humble way and extend it to even those you pass on the street. The Blessed Mother has given us a great gift and She desires us to use it.

(See the September 1988 Newsletter from Caritas of Birmingham, Box 120, 4647 Highway 280 East, Birmingham, Alabama 35242. This newsletter records the first public announcement about this SPECIAL BLESSING. The December-February 1988 issue also contains additional information.)

November 30, 1988, 10:30 p.m.

Our Lady came and was very happy. She blessed and prayed over everyone. Marija recommended all those present to Our Lady and She prayed The Lord's Prayer and the Glory Be. Our Lady extended Her arms and prayed in Hebrew over everyone. Her message:

"I wish that all your life be love, only love. Everything that you do, do it with love. In every little thing, see Jesus and His example. You also do as Jesus did. He died out of love for you. You also offer all you do with love to God, even the smallest little things of everyday life."

Then Our Lady made the Sign of the Cross and left saying, "Go in peace."

December 1, 1988, 10:30 a.m.

Our Lady came and was very happy. With her hands extended, she prayed over everyone and blessed them. All present, especially the sick, were recommended to Our Lady by Marija and Our Lady prayed The Lord's Prayer and the Glory Be. Our Lady also blessed the religious objects which were brought to the site. She made the Sign of the Cross and as She returned to heaven, Our Lady said, "Go in peace." No special message.

December 2, 1988, 10:30 p.m.

Our Lady came and was very happy. She prayed over everyone. She smiled and prayed "one by one" over each of the persons present in the room. Marija recommended all those present to Our Lady. She prayed The Lord's Prayer and the Glory Be. The message:

"I invite you to pray and to abandon yourself totally to God."

Our Lady then made the Sign of the Cross and went away saying, "Go in peace."

December 3, 1988, 10:30 p.m.

Our Lady came and was very happy. Marija recommended all those present to Our Lady. Marija asked Our Lady if She would pray over each individual as she had done yesterday. Very pleased, Our Lady smiled. She looked at everyone and began to pray over each one individually with Her hands over them. Our Lady prayed The Lord's Prayer and the Glory Be. The message:

"Dear children, I give you my love, so you give it to others."

Marija asked if Our Lady would appear tomorrow in the morning. Our Lady smiled and said,

"Yes, at 10:40 as in Medjugorje."

(The time, 10:40 a.m. Central Time, corresponds to same moment of the apparition in Medjugorje.)

Then Our Lady made the Sign of the Cross saying, **"Go in peace,"** and She left. Marija's voice was beautiful, gentle, full of love and intensity when she talked about the apparition just after Our Lady left. All felt Our Lady's presence and sensed that She was happy in a special way.

December 4, 1988, 10:40 a.m.

Our Lady came and She was very happy. Marija recommended all those present to Our Lady, especially the sick. Our Lady prayed over everyone and she blessed them all. She prayed The Lord's Prayer and the Glory Be. The message:

> **"I invite you to live the profoundness of the messages that I give."**

Our Lady also blessed the objects. She made the Sign of the Cross while leaving saying, **"Go in peace."**

December 5, 1988, 10:40 a.m.

Our Lady came and She was very happy. Marija recommended all the people present to Her. Our Lady extended Her hands and prayed over everyone and said The Lord's Prayer and the Glory Be. She left saying, **"Go in peace."** No special message.

Marija left to go back to Medjugorje for one week to inform her family and priest about the operation. She returned to the host's home near Birmingham on December 12, 1988.

December 13, 1988

Today there was an apparition but no public message.

Father Robert Faricy was present during the apparitions on December 13 and 14, 1988. He was amazed and said:

"I visited Marija in Birmingham and prayed with her and the others when Our Lady came to her in the bedroom. Not even in Medjugorje did I feel so strongly Mary's presence as I did during Her apparition to Marija in Birmingham."

December 14, 1988, 10:40 a.m.

"I would like you to pray for my intentions."

She left saying, **"Go in peace."**

December 15, 1988, 10:40 a.m.

"Dear children, I love you and I wish you to pray for my intentions with the love you have for me, so that every plan of God about each one of you may be fulfilled."

Referring to Marija's operation, Our Lady said:

"I will be with you tomorrow."

December 16, 1988

Today Marija underwent surgery after test results showed that she could donate her kidney to her brother, Andrija. During the operation, with rosary in her hand and while under anesthesia, Our Lady appeared over Marija while she lay on the operating table. Marija later said Our Lady stayed with her and smiled for what seemed to her about two hours. For the next month, except for Christmas Eve, Our Lady did not speak to Marija. She appeared to her each day at Mass during Communion. January 15, 1989, Our Lady told Marija that the next day She would again give messages. There was great joy in everyone's hearts.

December 24, 1988, (near midnight) (SPECIAL BLESSING)
(The monthly message):

The December 25, 1988 monthly message was actually given on
December 24, 1988, near midnight, and extended into Christmas Day.
The message:

> **"Dear children, I call you to peace. Live it in your heart and
> all around you so that all will know peace - peace which does
> not come from you but from God. Little children, today is a
> great day! Rejoice with me! Glorify the Nativity of Jesus
> through the peace that I give. It is for this peace that I have
> come as your Mother, Queen of Peace. Today I give you my
> Special Blessing. Bring it to all creation, so that all creation
> will know peace. Thank you for having responded to my call."**

December 25, 1988, 6:00 p.m.

Our Lady appeared again on Christmas Day during Mass in the loft
of the home where Marija was staying. Our Lady was robed in gold,
holding Baby Jesus in Her arms.

January 15, 1989

Our Lady appeared to Marija during Communion while Marija was
in the loft attending Mass which was being celebrated downstairs in
the home where she was staying. Our Lady said to Marija:

> **"Tomorrow, again, I will appear in the bedroom and give
> messages."**

January 16, 1989

Today Our Lady began to speak to Marija again. During this
apparition Our Lady, with a wonderful smile on Her face, blessed a
newborn baby making a Sign of the Cross in his direction. The
message:

"I call every one of you to live the messages I give and to witness by your lives."

January 17, 1989, 5:40 p.m.

"Pray for my intentions. With this prayer, I would like to help each one of you."

January 18, 1989, 5:40 p.m.

"Pray for my intentions."

January 19, 1989, 5:45 p.m.

"I ask you to pray and demand [ask boldly for] the graces from me. I will intercede in front of God for you."

January 20, 1989, 5:40 p.m.

No public message; however, Our Lady did give a private message for someone in the room.

January 21, 1989, 5:40 p.m.

"I am calling you to prayer; only through prayer can you come close to God. I am calling you to pray every day and to dedicate a special time in your day only for prayer."

January 22, 1989, 5:40 p.m.

"I wish you to pray for my intentions. Only in this way can you come closer to God. I will guide you to Him. Pray, dear children, I am with you."

January 23, 1989, 5:40 p.m.

"I would like you to pray for my intentions."

Again, Our Lady gave a private message.

January 24, 1989

Today Marija was late for the apparition and couldn't get to the home at the appointed time. Our Lady came to her but gave no special message; however, Our Lady did say that She extended Her blessing and received all the intentions of the several thousand people who were present near the tree.

January 25, 1989, 10:40 a.m.
(The Monthly Message)

"Dear children, today I am calling you to the way of holiness. Pray that you may comprehend the beauty and the greatness of this way, where God reveals Himself to you in a special way. Pray that you may be open to everything that God does through you so that in your life you may be enabled to give thanks to God and to rejoice over everything that He does through each individual. I give you my blessing. Thank you for your response to my call."

January 26, 1989, 10:40 a.m.

"Dear children, I desire that your lives becomes prayer."

Marija said that Our Lady was always very happy. Marija flew to Italy and convalesced for another two months before returning to Medjugorje.

CHAPTER 6

THE INTERIOR LOCUTION MESSAGES FROM OUR LADY TO JELENA AND MARIJANA

(February, 1982 to July 30, 1987)

Jelena Vasilj and Marijana Vasilj are two young girls (not related) who, after the apparitions occurred to the six visionaries, would pray to Our Lady while others their age would be out playing. One day they heard the voice of Our Lady and saw Her in an interior way. These interior apparitions have continued since that time. While they are different from the apparitions of the six visionaries whose messages are more general in nature, these messages are stronger in detail and of great value.

Jelena hears and sees Our Lady with the heart. She sees Our Lady as if in a movie, in two dimensions. Our Lady appears to her and to Marijana wearing a white dress. Marijana sees and hears Our Lady in the same manner.

The following messages have been given to Jelena unless otherwise stated.

The End of February-Beginning of March, 1982

To Jelena:

"**Dear children, if you knew how much I love you, your heart would cry.**"

"**If there is someone there who asks you for something, give it to him.**"

"I also stand in front of many hearts, and they do not open up. Pray so that the world may welcome my love."

"Dear children, I would like for the whole world to be my child, but it does not want it. I wish to give everything for the world. For that, Pray!"

April 4, 1982 - April 10, 1982

Jelena asked Our Lady about the meaning of her vision. She saw Jesus being held by the hand by Mary. There were many words written on the arm and palm of Jesus' hand. Jelena could read the inscription, "Glory," on the palm of Jesus' hand.

"These are the names of all those who have been inscribed in the heart of Jesus."

December 29, 1982

Jelena asks if the ten secrets may be revealed to her:

"I do not appear to you as to the other six because my plan is different. To them I entrusted messages and secrets. Forgive me if I cannot tell you the secrets which I have entrusted to them. This is a grace which is for them, but not for you. I appeared to you for the purpose of helping you to progress in spiritual life and through your intermediary I want to lead people to holiness."

Beginning of 1983

Jelena asked Our Lady about the authenticity of the apparitions received by the six visionaries and about the date of the sign which She promised to send:

"Pardon me, but you cannot know it; it is a special gift for them. You will have to believe it like all the others. In the meantime, everything that they say corresponds to truth."

March 1, 1983

"Transcribe all the lessons which I give you for the spiritual life; later you will deliver them to the authorities of the Church."

April 4, 1983

Jelena delivers a message to Father Tomislav Vlasic regarding problems in his parish which she was not aware of. Jelena says: "Do not have recourse to anyone. When you have a problem, you must remain smiling and praying. When God begins a work, no one will stop it."

Our Lady said:

"Pray, fast, and allow God to act."

"Do not pity anyone. If the police cause you some anxiety, continue on your way joyful and calm. Pray for them. When God begins His work, no one can stop it."

According to Father Vlasic, these internal locutions were received by Jelena after December 15, 1982:

"Hurry to be converted. Do not wait for the great sign. For the unbelievers, it will then be too late to be converted. For you who have the faith, this time constitutes a great opportunity for you to be converted, and to deepen your faith. Fast on bread and water before every feast, and prepare yourselves through prayer.

"Fast once a week on bread and water in honor of the Holy Spirit outside of Friday.

"Have the largest possible number of persons pray and fast during the Novena of the Holy Spirit, so that it may spread over the Church. Fast and pray for the Bishop."

April 20, 1983

In tears Our Lady said to Jelena:

"I give all the graces to those who commit grave sins, but they
do not convert. Pray! Pray for them! Do not wait for Friday.
Pray now. Today your prayers and your penance are necessary
to me."

April 25, 1983

"Be converted! It will be too late when the sign comes.
Beforehand, several warnings will be given to the world. Hurry
to be converted. I need your prayers and your penance."

"My heart is burning with love for you. For you it is enough
to be converted. To ask questions is unimportant. Be
converted. Hurry to proclaim it. Tell everyone that it is my
wish, and that I do not cease repeating it. Be converted, be
converted. It is not difficult for me to suffer for you. I beg
you, be converted.

"I will pray to my Son to spare you the punishment. Be
converted without delay. You do not know the plans of God;
you will not be able to know them. You will not know what
God will send, nor what He will do. I ask you only to be
converted. That is what I wish. Be converted! Be ready for
everything, but be converted. That is part of conversion.
Goodbye, and may peace be with you."

April 29, 1983

Jelena asks Our Lady why both Marijana (aged 11) and she see
Our Lady but Marijana does not hear Her words:

"I do not want to separate you."

(Does this suggest that Our Lady is saying that these two girls complete each other?) Also, Our Lady respects their friendship.

May 25, 1983

"Assemble about twenty young people who are ready to follow Jesus without reservation. Bring them together within a month's notice. I will initiate them into the spiritual life. There can even be more than twenty. Even some adults and children can participate, all those who will accept the rule.

"I will ask these people to do penance for certain intentions. They will fast and pray for the Bishop. They will give up what they cherish the most: drink, coffee, pleasures, television. It is necessary to have persons who wish to consecrate themselves to religious life. Others have to be ready to consecrate themselves specially to prayer and fasting. I will give them rules to follow.

"The persons who will follow these rules, will be consecrated whatever their state in life may be."

May 28, 1983

"It is very beautiful to remain Thursdays for the adoration of my Son in the Blessed Sacrament of the Altar. It is likewise beautiful to venerate the crucifix each Friday. I wish that every Saturday, which is the day that the Church had dedicated to me, you will consecrate to me at least a quarter of an hour. Meditate during this time, on my life, my messages, and pray."

June 10, 1983

After an argument, two of the three involved, Jelena and Marijana, reconcile and enter the church. When the third girl, Anita, enters the church she suddenly extends her hand to the others who become filled with joy. Our Lady says:

"I had been waiting for quite a while for your success. Continue in this manner."

June 16, 1983

Our Lady dictates the rules for the prayer group which will be totally abandoned to Jesus to Jelena:

1. "Renounce all passions and all inordinate desires. Avoid television, particularly evil programs, excessive sports, the unreasonable enjoyment of food and drink, alcohol, tobacco, etc.

2. "Abandon yourselves to God without any restrictions.

3. "Definitely eliminate all anguish. Whoever abandons himself to God does not have room in his heart for anguish. Difficulties will persist, but they will serve for spiritual growth and will render glory to God.

4. "Love your enemies. Banish from your heart hatred, bitterness, preconceived judgments. Pray for your enemies and call the Divine blessing over them.

5. "Fast twice a week on bread and water. Join the group at least once a week.

6. "Devote at least three hours to prayer daily, of which at least is half an hour in the morning and half an hour in the evening. Holy Mass and the prayer of the Rosary are included in this time of prayer. Set aside moments of prayer in the course of the day, and each time that circumstances permit it, receive Holy Communion. Pray with great meditation. Do not look at your watch all the time, but allow yourself to be lead by the grace of God. Do not concern yourself too much with the things of this world, but entrust all that in prayer to Our Heavenly Father. If one is very

preoccupied, he will not be able to pray well because internal serenity is lacking. God will contribute to lead to a successful end the things of here below if one strives to work for God's things.

"Those who attend school or go to work must pray half an hour in the morning and in the evening, and, if possible, participate in the Eucharist. It is necessary to extend the spirit of prayer to daily work, that is to say, to accompany work with prayer.

7. "Be prudent because the devil tempts all those who have made a resolution to consecrate themselves to God, most particularly, those people. He will suggest to them that they are praying too much, they are fasting too much, that they must be like other young people and go in search of pleasures. Have them not listen to him, nor obey him. It is to the voice of the Blessed Virgin that they should pay attention. When they will be strengthened in their faith, the devil will no longer be able to seduce them.

8. "Pray very much for the Bishop and for those who hold positions in the Church. No less than half of their prayers and sacrifices must be devoted to this intention."

Our Lady tells Jelena:

"I have come to tell the world that God is truth; He exists. True happiness and the fullness of life are in Him. I have come here as Queen of Peace to tell the world that peace is necessary for the salvation of the world. In God, one finds true joy from which true peace is derived."

The Spring of 1983

Regarding Anita to whom Our Lady appeared but who is rarely able to join Jelena and Marijana because of her duties, Our Lady said to Jelena:

> **"If she cannot come because of her obligations, have her pray for a quarter of an hour at least, and I will appear to her and bless her."**

June 22, 1983

> **"Love your enemies and bless them!"**

June 28, 1983

> **"Pray for three hours a day. You don't pray enough. Pray at least a half hour in the morning and in the evening."**

July 2, 1983

> **"Devote five minutes to the Sacred Heart. Each family is an image of it."**

July 4, 1983

> **"You have begun to pray three hours a day, but you look at your watch, preoccupied with your work. Be preoccupied with only the essential. Let yourself be guided by the Holy Spirit in depth, then your work will go well. Do not hurry. Let yourself be guided and you will see that everything will be accomplished well."**

July 26, 1983

> **"Be on your guard. This period is dangerous for you. The devil is trying to lead you astray from the way. Those who give themselves to God will be the object of attacks."**

August 2, 1983

"Consecrate yourself to the Immaculate Heart. Abandon yourselves completely. I will protect you. I will pray to the Holy Spirit. Pray to Him also."

August 15, 1983

"See how I am happy here! There are many who honor me. In the meanwhile, do not forget that in other places there are still more persons who hurt me and offend me."

"Do not be in anxiety. May peace unite your hearts. Every disorder comes from Satan."

Regarding the youth who are going back to school:

"Be careful not to diminish the spirit of prayer."

"Satan is enraged against those who fast and those who are converted."

September 16, 1983

This message was given to Jelena for the Pope:

"Pray, pray, pray! Do not be discouraged. Be in peace because God gives you the grace to defeat Satan."

"In my messages, I recommend to everyone, and to the Holy Father in particular, to spread the message which I have received from my Son here at Medjugorje. I wish to entrust to the Pope the word with which I came here: 'MIR'(peace), which he must spread everywhere. Here is a message which is especially for him: That he bring together the Christian people through his word and his preaching; that he spread, particularly among the young people, the messages which he has received from the Father in his prayer, when God inspires him."

September 29, 1983

"I desire for a great peace and a great love to grow in you. Consequently, Pray!"

Regarding three priests from Liverpool:

"Preach my messages. Speak about the events at Medjugorje. Continue to increase your prayers."

Autumn, 1983

"Dear children, one lives not only from work. One lives also from prayer."* [See endnote, page 330.]

October 20, 1983

To Jelena for the prayer group:

"I ask you for a commitment of four years. It is not yet the time to choose your vocation. The important thing is, first of all, to enter into prayer. Later, you will make the right choice."

To Jelena for the parish:

"May all the families consecrate themselves to the Sacred Heart each day. I am very happy when the entire family meets to pray each morning for half and hour."

October 24, 1983

For the prayer group:

"If you pray, a source of life will flow from your hearts. If you pray with strength, if you pray with faith, you will receive graces from this source, and your group will be strengthened."

October 25, 1983

"Pray! Pray! Prayer will give you everything. It is with prayer that you can obtain everything."

October 26, 1983

"I pour out my blessing over you, and my heart wishes to be with you."

October 27, 1983

"Pray, pray, pray. You will get nothing from chatter, but only from prayer. If someone asks you about me, and about what I say, answer: 'It is no use to explain. It is in praying that we will understand better.'"

October 28, 1983

"I see that you are tired. I wish to support you in your effort, to take you in my arms so that you may be close to me. To all those who wish to ask me questions, I will answer: 'There is only one response, prayer, a strong faith, and intense prayer, and fasting.'"

October 29, 1983

"I give you my heart; accept it! I would not want to distress you, nor to stop talking to you, but I cannot stay always with you. You have to get used to it. In the meantime, I wish to be constantly with you, with the heart. It is necessary to pray much, not to say: 'If today we have not prayed, it is nothing serious.'

"You must strive to pray. Prayer is the only road which leads to peace. If you pray and fast, you will obtain everything that you ask for."

October 30, 1983

"Why do you not put your trust in me? I know that you have been praying for a long time but really surrender yourself. Abandon your concerns to Jesus. Listen to what He says in the Gospel: 'And who among you, through his anxiety, is able to add a single cubit to the length of his life.' (Mt. 6:27).

"Pray also, in the evening when you have finished your day. Sit down in your room, and say to Jesus: 'Thank you.'

"If in the evening you fall asleep in peace and in prayer, in the morning you will wake up thinking of Jesus. You will then be able to pray for peace; but if you fall asleep in distraction, the day after will be misty, and you will forget even to pray that day."

October 31, 1983

"I know that you prayed today, and that you did all your work while praying. Still, I have a particular intention for which I am asking you to say each day the Lord's Prayer seven times, seven Hail Mary's, and the Creed."

November 4, 1983

"I wish that you tell them that tomorrow is a day of fasting in order to sanctify yourselves in the Holy Spirit. And pray! Let this message be conveyed to the group."

November 5, 1983

"I know, my children, that you have worked and prayed today. But, I beseech you, be generous, persevere, continue to pray."

November 6, 1983

"Where are the prayers which you used to address to me? My clothes were sparkling. Behold them soaked with tears. Oh, if you would know how the world today is plunged into sin. It seems to you that the world sins no longer, because here, you live in a peaceful world where there is neither confusion nor perversity.

"If you knew how lukewarm they are in their faith, how many do not listen to Jesus, oh, if you knew how much I suffer, you would sin no more. Oh, how I need your prayers. Pray!"

November 7, 1983

"Do not go to confession through habit, to remain the same after it. No, it is not good. Confession should give an impulse to your faith. It should stimulate you and bring you closer to Jesus. If confession does not mean anything for you, really, you will be converted with great difficulty."

November 8, 1983

"Pray and fast! All that you can do for me is to pray and fast."

November 9, 1983

"Pray! I have such a great need for your prayers. Give me your hearts."

November 10, 1983

"I ask you to pray. That is all that I expect of you. Do not forget to pray to the Lord, morning and evening. Pray, Pray."

November 11, 1983

"Pray! You can do everything; yes, you can do it through prayer. Place an image of the hearts of Jesus and Mary in your homes."

November 12, 1983

"Give me your hearts, open them to me."

In response to the question, "How?" Our Lady says:

"You must redouble your efforts. Day after day, increase your fervor."

November 13, 1983

"Pray, and do it with fervor. Include the whole world in your prayer. Pray, because prayer makes one live."

When asked a question, Our Lady said:

"Pray and you will understand that some day."

November 14, 1983

"Pray, because prayer is life. Through it and in it, you live in prayer."

November 15, 1983

"Pray and fast!"

Regarding an intention of the group:

"I have often reproached you. Pray with me. Begin right now."

November 16, 1983

"Pray and fast. May all the members of your group come on Tuesday if they can. Speak to them about fasting. Fast three days a week for the Bishop. If that cannot be done by everyone the same day, have each one do it whenever he is able."

November 17, 1983

"Pray! If I always ask you to pray, do not think that your prayers are not good. But I invite you to prolong your personal prayer, to pray more intensely for the others."

November 18, 1983

"In Medjugorje, many have begun well, but they have turned toward material goods, and they forget the only good."

November 19, 1983

"My children, pray only!"

November 20, 1983

"My children, do not believe everything that people tell you. One must not, because it weakens ones faith."

November 21, 1983

"Tuesday, that is tomorrow, the whole group will find peace in prayer. All its members will be invigorated in prayer, as it is the wish of Jesus. He entrusts something to each one, and wishes something from each one. It is necessary to make them come back to their promises, which were made at the beginning, and to pray."

November 22, 1983

"Pray, pray, pray. . . . Pray, my children. Pray, because only prayer can save you."

November 23, 1983

"Oh my sweet children, pray! I ask you only to pray. You yourselves can see that only prayer can save."

November 24, 1983

"Pray and fast!"

November 25, 1983

"Pray and fast."

November 26, 1983

"Prayer and fasting."

November 27, 1983

"My children, pray and keep your soul pure. I wish to be constantly with you."

November 28, 1983

"Pray, pray! Have the parish pray each day to the hearts of Jesus and Mary during the Novena of the Immaculate Conception."

The following prayers were given on this same day:

CONSECRATION TO THE HEART OF JESUS

O Jesus, we know that You are sweet (Mt. 11:29),
That You have given Your Heart for us.
It was crowned with thorns by our sins.
We know that today You still pray for us
so that we will not be lost.
Jesus, remember us if we fall into sin.
Through Your most Sacred Heart,
make us all love one another.
Cause hatred to disappear among men.
Show us Your love.
All of us love You.
And we desire that you protect us with Your
Heart of the Good Shepherd.
Enter into each heart, Jesus!
Knock on the door of our hearts.
Be patient and tenacious with us.
We are still locked up in ourselves, because we
have not understood Your will.
Knock continuously, Oh Jesus.
Make our hearts open up to you,
at least when we remember the passion
which you suffered for us. Amen.

CONSECRATION TO THE
IMMACULATE HEART OF MARY

O Immaculate Heart of Mary, overflowing
with goodness, Show us your love for us.
May the flame of your heart, Oh Mary,
Descend upon all peoples.
We love you immensely.
Impress in our hearts a true love.
May our hearts yearn for you.
Oh Mary, sweet and humble of heart,
Remember us when we sin.
You know that we men are sinners.

Through your most sacred and maternal heart,
Cure us from every spiritual illness.
Make us capable of looking at the beauty
of your maternal heart,
And that, thus, we may be converted
to the flame of your heart. Amen.

November 29, 1983

"Pray!"

For the group's intentions:

"I am your mother full of goodness, and Jesus is your great friend. Do not fear anything in His presence. Give Him your heart. From the bottom of your heart tell Him your sufferings, thus you will be invigorated in prayer, with a free heart, in a peace without fear."

November 30, 1983

"Pray, pray, pray!"

November, 1983

The Blessed Virgin tells Jelena that the Mass should always be accompanied by prayers to the Holy Spirit:

"Before Mass it is necessary to pray to the Holy Spirit."

December 1, 1983

Thanks to all of you who have come here, so numerous during this year, in spite of snow, ice and bad weather, to pray to Jesus. Continue, hold on in your suffering. You know well that when a friend asks you for something, you give it to him. It is thus with Jesus. When you pray without ceasing, and you come in spite of your tiredness, He will give you all that you ask from Him. For that, pray."

December 2, 1983

"Thank you, thanks to everyone!"

Regarding the cold evening:

"Be kind to come to Mass without looking for an excuse. Show me that you have a generous heart."

December 4, 1983

"Pray, pray, pray only. Prayer should be for you not only a habit but also a source of happiness. You should live by prayer."

December 6, 1983

"Pray, pray! If you pray, I will keep you and I will be with you."

December 7, 1983 (VIGIL OF IMMACULATE CONCEPTION)

"Tomorrow will really be a blessed day for you, if every moment is consecrated to my Immaculate Heart. Abandon yourselves to me. Strive to make your joy grow, to live in the faith, to change your hearts."

December 8, 1983

"Thank you my children for coming in such large numbers. Thank you. Continue your efforts and be persevering and tenacious. Pray without ceasing."

December 11, 1983

"Pray and fast! I wish that prayer be renewed in your heart every day. Pray more, yes, more each day."

December 12, 1983

"Pray, pray, thus I will protect you. Pray and abandon your hearts to me, because I wish to be with you."

December 13, 1983

"Pray and fast! I do not wish to say anything else to you."

December 14, 1983

"Pray and fast! I am asking you for prayer."

December 15, 1983

"Fast on Thursday and Friday for the Bishop."

Regarding catastrophic predictions:

"That comes from false prophets. They say: 'Such a day, on such a date, there will be a catastrophe.' I have always said that misfortune will come if the world does not convert itself. Call the world to conversion. Everything depends on your conversion."

December 16, 1983

"Pray and fast only!"

December 17, 1983

"Pray and fast!"

December 18, 1983

"In this novena for Christmas, pray as much as you can. I ask you."

December 19, 1983

"Pray!"

December 20, 1983

"Pray!"

For the group's intention"

"Fast on Wednesday, Thursday, and Friday."

December 21, 1983

"My children, I say to you again, pray and fast."

December 22, 1983

"Pray! What is most important for your body is prayer."

December 23, 1983

"Pray, pray, especially tomorrow. I desire your prayers."

December 24, 1983

"Pray, pray my children. I wish that this night be spent in prayer."

December 25, 1983

> "My children, pray! I cannot tell you anything else than pray.
> Know that in your life, there is nothing more important than
> prayer."

December 26, 1983

> "My children, pray. Pray again. Do not say: 'Our Lady only
> repeats, pray.' I cannot tell you anything else than to pray.
> You needed to live this Christmas in prayer. You have
> rejoiced very much this Christmas, but your hearts have not
> attained and lived what you have desired. No one withdrew to
> his room to thank Jesus."

December 27, 1983

> "My children, pray, pray, pray. Remember that the most
> important thing in our lives is prayer."

December 28, 1983

> "My children, understand that the most important thing in our
> lives is prayer."

December 29, 1983

> "I wish that one love, one peace, flourish in you. Therefore,
> pray."

December 30, 1983

> "My children, pray and fast. I wish to strengthen you, but
> prayer alone is your strength."

December 31, 1983

"For you, I only wish that this new year will really be a holy one. On this day, go then to confession and purify yourself in this new year.

Prayers for the Bishop were requested of the group.

1983

"When others cause you some difficulty, do not defend it, rather, pray."

1983

"I desire that you be a flower, which blossoms for Jesus at Christmas, a flower which does not cease to bloom when Christmas has passed. I wish that you have a shepherd's heart for Jesus."

"Dear children, when someone comes to you and asks you a favor, answer by giving. I find myself before so many hearts which do not open themselves to me. Pray, so that the world willingly wants to accept my love."

1983

"Take me seriously. When God comes among men, he does not come to joke but to say serious things.

"It is better to stay in church and pray with faith than to gather together with onlookers near the seers during an apparition."* [See endnote, page 330.]

January 1, 1984

"My children, pray! I say again, pray, because prayer is indispensable to life."

January 2, 1984

Jelena's prayer group thought they could stop saying the prayer to the Holy Spirit, thinking Our Lady only wanted it said until Christmas.

"Why have you stopped saying the prayer to the Holy Spirit? I have asked you to pray always and at all times so that the Holy Spirit may descend over all of you. Begin again to pray for that."

January 3, 1984

"My children, pray; I say it again, pray! Know that in your life the most important thing is prayer."

January 4, 1984

"Before all, pray; I say it again, pray! Know that in your life the most important thing is prayer."

January 8, 1984

"My children, pray! I say it again, pray! I will say it to you again. Do not think that Jesus is going to manifest Himself again in the manger; friends, He is born again in your hearts."

January 15, 1984

"I know that I speak to you very often about prayer; but know that there are many people in the world who do not pray, who do not even know what to say in prayer."

January 17, 1984

"Pray and fast! I wish that in your hearts prayer and fasting flourish."

January 18, 1984

"I wish to engrave in every heart the sign of love. If you love all mankind, then there is peace in you. If you are at peace with all men, it is the kingdom of love."

"Pray and fast!"

For the group's intention:

"Have everyone get up early, some to go to school, others to go to work, still others to help the poor like themselves, also those who need help."

January 19, 1984

"Pray and fast, because without prayer you cannot do anything."

January 21, 1984

"Pray and fast. Do not give up on meditation. At home meditate at least half an hour."

January 22, 1984

"Pray and fast. I permit all those who want to make a sacrifice to fast, at the most, three times a week. May they not prolong it."

January 23, 1984

"Pray and fast. You have not understood well, what it means to pray. May you understand that; I desire it very much."

January 24, 1984

"Pray much. I desire to permeate [saturate] you with prayer."

January 25, 1984

"Pray and fast. You need vigor (or strength) in your prayer. May you pray in recollection for a long time and fervently."

January 26, 1984

"Thank you for adoring my Son in the Sacred Host. That touches me very much. As for you, pray! I desire to see you happy."

January 27, 1984

"Pray and fast. I wish that you always deepen your life in prayer. Every morning say the Prayer of Consecration to the Heart of Mary. Do it in family. Recite each morning the Angelus (once), The Lord's Prayer, the Hail Mary, and the Glory Be five times in honor of the Holy Passion, and a sixth time for our Holy Father, the Pope. Then say the Creed and the Prayer to the Holy Spirit; and, if it is possible, it would be well to pray one part of the Rosary."

January 28, 1984

"I wish that all of you pray, and that my heart extends to the whole world. I wish to be with you."

January 29, 1984

"Pray and fast! I wish for you to purify your hearts. Purify them and open them to me."

January 30, 1984

"Pray! I desire to purify your hearts. Pray. It is indispensable, because God gives you the greatest graces when you pray."

January 31, 1984

"Pray! Do not think of anything, pray. Do not think of anything else except of those for whom you pray. Then prayer will be better and you will be faithful to it."

For the group:

"Continue to help the poor, the sick, and to pray for the dead. You should not feel any fear. Let all free themselves completely and let them abandon their hearts to me so that I can be with them. Have them listen to me and discover me in the poor, and in every man."

February 1, 1984

"It is raining at this time, and you say: 'It is not reasonable to go to church in this slush. Why is it raining so much?' Do not ever speak like that. You have not ceased to pray so that God may send you rain which makes the earth rich. Then do not turn against the blessing from God. Above all, thank Him through prayer and fasting."

February 2, 1984

"Pray, because I need more prayers. Be reconciled, because I desire reconciliation among you and more love for each other, like brothers. I wish that prayer, peace, and love bloom in you."

February 3, 1984

Regarding questions to Our Lady about the diary of Vicka which arrived from the Bishop on January 13, 1984:

"It is up to you to pray and I will take care of the rest. You cannot even imagine how powerful God is. That is why, pray!

Pray because he wants to be with you and wants to cleanse you from all sin."

February 4, 1984

"Pray, because prayer is very necessary to you. With prayer, your body and soul will find peace. There are some young people who have consecrated themselves to me. But there are in the parish some persons who are not entirely consecrated. As soon as Mass has ended, they are in a hurry to leave the church. That is not good. That way they will never be able to give themselves completely. It is not good for them to linger about the church. One must be pious and set a good example for others, in order to awaken in them the faith. It is necessary to pray as much as possible while offering your heart. One has to consecrate himself if he wants to be truly better."

February 5, 1984

"Pray and fast. I desire to live in your hearts."

Especially for the Prayer Group:

"Some of them still have a week of rest. They do not fast . . . others have come here and fast on Wednesday, Thursday, and Friday. Others help the poor and the sick. Others love everybody and want to discover Jesus in each one. Some are not convinced, others are. Those are mine. See how they honor me. Lead them to me so that I may bless them."

February 6, 1984

"Pray, pray, I ask of you."

February 8, 1984

From you, I expect only prayer. Thus, pray."

February 9, 1984

"Pray, pray! How many persons have followed other beliefs or sects and have abandoned Jesus Christ! They create their own gods; they adore idols. How that hurts me! If they could be converted! How unbelievers are in large numbers! That will change only if you help me with your prayers."

February 10, 1984

"Pray and fast! I desire humility from you; but you can become humble only through prayer and fasting."

February 11, 1984

"Open your hearts to me, I desire to bless them fully."

February 12, 1984

"I ask of you to pray and fast! Pray for the peace and humility of your hearts."

February 13, 1984

"Fast and pray! Give me your hearts. I desire to change them completely. I desire for them to be pure."

February 14, 1984

"Pray and fast! I desire you to purify your hearts completely. I wish to make you happy."

February 15, 1984

Regarding a very strong, icy wind blowing which everyone noticed on the way to Church:

"The wind is my sign. I will come in the wind. When the wind blows, know that I am with you. You have learned that the cross represents Christ; it is a sign of Him. It is the same for the crucifix you have in your home. For me, it is not the same. When it is cold, you come to church; you want to offer everything to God. I am, then, with you. I am with you in the wind. Do not be afraid."

February 17, 1984

"My children, pray! The world has been drawn into a great whirlpool. It does not know what it is doing. It does not realize in what sin it is sinking. It needs your prayers so that I can pull it out of this danger."

February 20, 1984

"Pray and fast! I desire to purify you and to save you. For that, help me with your prayers."

February 21, 1984

"Pray and fast! I expect generosity and prayer from your hearts."

February 23, 1984

"I hold all of you in my arms. You are mine. I need your prayers so that you may be all mine. I desire to be all yours and for you to be all mine. I receive all your prayers. I receive them with joy."

February 24, 1984

"Pray and fast! I desire to be with you always. I desire to stay in your hearts always and for you to stay in mine."

February 25, 1984

"Know that I love all of you. Know that you are all mine. To
no one do I desire to give more than to you. Come to me all
of you. Stay with me. I want to be your Mother. Come, I
desire all of you."

February 26, 1984

"Pray and fast! Know that I love you. I hold all of you on my
knees."

February 27, 1984

"Do not be tired. I desire to be with you."

February 28, 1984

"Pray and fast! Love everyone on earth, just as you love
yourselves."

For the intention of the prayer group:

"Have each one decide alone. In the meantime it would be
good that this week they fast on Thursday. Have them read
the Bible and meditate on it."

February 29, 1984

"Pray! It may seem strange to you that I always speak of
prayer, and yet I say: pray! Why do you hesitate? In Holy
Scripture you have heard it said, 'Do not worry about
tomorrow, each day will have its own worries.' Then do not
worry about the other days. Be content with prayer. I, your
Mother, will take care of the rest."

March 1, 1984

To Marijana:

> "Pray and fast. When I tell you to pray, do not think that you have to pray more, but pray. Let prayer and faith awaken in your hearts."

To Jelena:

> "Each Thursday, read again the passage of Matthew 6:24-34, before the Most Blessed Sacrament, or if it is not possible to come to church, do it with your family."

March 5, 1984

> "Pray and fast! Ask the Holy Spirit to renew your souls, to renew the entire world."

March 17, 1984

In preparation for the feast of the Annunciation:

> "Pray and fast, so that during this novena, God will fill you with His Power."

March 21, 1984

> "Today I rejoice with all my angels. The first part of my program has been achieved."

Crying:

> "There are so many men who live in sin. Here there are likewise among you some people who have offended my heart. Pray and fast for them."

March 22, 1984

"Yesterday evening I said that the first wish of my plan was realized."

March 27, 1984

"In the group, some have given themselves up to God so that He may guide them. Allow the will of God be realized in you."

March 30, 1984

"My children, I wish that the Holy Mass be for you the gift of the day. Attend it, wish for it to begin. Jesus gives Himself to you during the Mass. Thus, look forward to that moment when you are cleansed. Pray very much so that the Holy Spirit will renew your parish. If people attend Mass with lukewarmness, they will return to their homes cold, and with an empty heart."

April 3, 1984

"I ask for you to pray for the conversion of all men. For that, I need your prayers."

April 14, 1984

"How can you not be happy? Jesus gives Himself to you. I wish to inundate souls. If I am sad this evening, the reason is that many have not prepared themselves for Easter. They do not permit Jesus on that day to unite Himself to their souls."

April 15, 1984 - April 22, 1984 (HOLY WEEK)

"Raise your hands and open your hearts. Now, at the time of the Resurrection, Jesus wishes to give you a special gift. This gift of my Son is my gift. Here it is. You will be subjected to trials and you will endure them with great ease. We will be

ready to show you how to escape from them if you accept us.
Do not say that the Holy Year has ended and that there is no
need to pray. On the contrary, double your prayers because
the Holy Year is just another step ahead."

The Risen Jesus, with rays of light coming forth from His wounds,
appeared and said:

"Receive my graces and tell the whole world that there is no
happiness except through Me."

April 19, 1984

Our Lady dictated this prayer to Jelena:

HOW TO GIVE ONESELF TO MARY
MOTHER OF GOODNESS, OF LOVE AND OF MERCY

Oh my Mother!
Mother of goodness, love and mercy!
I love you immensely, and I offer myself to you.
Through your goodness, your love,
And your mercy, save me!
I wish to be yours.
I love you immensely
And I wish that you protect me.
In my heart, oh mother of goodness,
Give me your goodness,
So that I go to Heaven.
I ask you for your immense love
That you may give me the grace
That I will be able to love each one
Just like you loved Jesus Christ.
I ask you in grace
That I be able to be merciful to you.
I offer myself completely to you
And I wish that you will be with me at each step,
Because you are full of grace.

I wish never to forget your grace,
And if I should lose it,
I will ask, make me find it again. Amen.

Jelena asked Our Lady this question for Father Vlasic: "How could Jesus pray all night? With what method?" Our Lady said:

"He had a great longing for God and for the salvation of souls."

April 20, 1984

"You should be filled with joy. Today Jesus died for your salvation. He descends into Hell and opens the gates of paradise. Let joy reign in your hearts!

"When you pray, pray more. Prayer is a conversation with God. To pray means to listen to the Lord. Prayer is for me a service, because after it, all things become clear. Prayer leads to knowing happiness."

April 21, 1984

"Raise your hands, yearn for Jesus because in his Resurrection, he wants to fill you with graces. Be enthusiastic about the Resurrection. All of us in Heaven are happy, but we seek the joy of your hearts. My Son's gift and mine, at this moment is this: you will be comforted in your trials, they will be easier for you because we will be close to you. If you listen to us, we will show you how to overcome them.

"Pray much tomorrow. May Jesus truly rise in your families. Where there is war, may peace come. I wish that a new man would be born in your hearts. My children, I thank you. Continue to bring about the Resurrection of Jesus in all men. The Holy Year has ended, but it represents only a step in our life. Continue to pray."

April 24, 1984

"Many times, confronting justice and confronting your sins, many times I returned from your home in tears. I could not say a single word. I am your Mother and I do not want to oppose you. But what I shall do in you is up to you.

"We must rejoice in Jesus, to make Him happy."

May 19, 1984

"Dear children, at this time it is especially necessary for you to consecrate yourselves to me and to my heart. Love, pray, and fast."

May 21, 1984

"O dear children, how I wish that you would turn to me. See, my little children, it is the end of the school year and you have not even reached halfway. That is why now you must become a little more serious."

May 23, 1984

"I wish that the parish prepare itself through a novena, to receive the sacrament of Confirmation on the day of the feast of the Ascension."

May 25, 1984

"I truly wish that you would be pure on the day of Pentecost. Pray, pray that your spirit be changed on that day."

May 26, 1984

"Dear children, thank you for every prayer. Try to pray continuously, and do not forget that I love you and wish that all of you would love one another."

Regarding questions Jelena was requested to ask:

> "For all of these questions, there is an answer: pray to the
> Holy Spirit so that He may enlighten you, and you will come
> to know all that you wish."

May 28, 1984

> "Love is a gift from God. Therefore, pray that God may give
> you the gift to love."

May 30, 1984

> "The priests should visit families, more particularly those who
> do not practice anymore, and who have forgotten God. Priests
> should carry the Gospel of Jesus to the people, and teach them
> how to pray. And the priests themselves should pray more
> and also fast. They should give to the poor what they don't
> need."

May, 1984

Regarding the celebration of Our Lady's two thousandth birthday:

> "Throughout the centuries, I have given myself completely to
> you. Is it too much to give me, three days? Do not work on
> those days. Take your rosaries and pray. Fasting has been
> forgotten during the last quarter of the century within the
> Catholic Church."

Jelena tells Our Lady that if she tells the people to pray four hours
a day they will back out.

> "Don't you understand, that it is only one-sixth of the day?"

June 1, 1984

"May the love of God be always in you, because without it, you cannot be fully converted. Let the rosary in your hands make you think of Jesus.

"Dear children, strive to penetrate into the Mass, just as you should."

June 2, 1984

"Thank you for every prayer. Continue to pray, but pray with the heart. Dear children, again it is necessary for you to pray to the Holy Spirit and it would be good for you to pray The Lord's Prayer seven times in the church, as one does it for Pentecost."

During the Pentecost Novena, before each Our Father, the priest asks for one of the seven gifts of the Holy Spirit.

June 4, 1984

"Dear children, I am happy that you have begun to pray as I requested of you. Continue."

June 8, 1984

"Dear children, you need love. I have said it to you many times, and I remind you. Continue only to pray and be happy because I am with you."

June 11, 1984

"I wish that you continue to pray and to fast."

To the group:

> "I wish that you would become like a flower in the spring. The love which I give you is great, but sometimes you reject it, and thus, it becomes less. Always accept immediately the gifts which I give you so that you can profit from them."

Mid-June, 1984

> "Prepare yourselves through prayer for the third anniversary of the beginning of the apparitions. June 25th should be celebrated as the Feast of Mary, 'Queen of Peace.'"

June 21, 1984

> "If you knew how much I love you, you would cry with joy. When anyone is before you and asks you something, you will give it to him. I am before so many hearts, but they remain closed. Pray so that the world receives my love."

> "Each member of the group is like a flower; and if someone tries to crush you, you will grow and will try to grow even more. If someone crushes you a little, you will recover. And if someone pulls a petal, continue to grow as though you were complete."

To Marijana:

> "My only wish is that you become as joyful and enthusiastic as you were during the first days of my apparitions."

June 23, 1984

> "Dear children, I am very happy that there are so many people here this evening. Thank God alone."

August 2, 1984

"**Dear children, today I am joyful and I thank you for your prayers. Pray still more these days for the conversion of sinners. Thank you for having responded to my call.**"

After Easter, Our Lady speaks to Jelena or Marijana on Tuesdays, Wednesdays, Saturdays, and Sundays rather than everyday.

The Beginning of August, 1984

"**This message is dedicated to the Pope and to all Christians. Prepare the second millennium of my birth which will take place August 5, 1984. Throughout the centuries, I consecrated my entire life to you. Is it too much for you to consecrate three days for me? Do not work on that day, but take up the rosary and pray.**"

August 2, 1984

"**I am happy for your participation at Mass. Continue as you did this evening. Thank you for having resisted the temptation of Satan.**"

August, 1984

"**Christians make a mistake in considering the future because they think of wars and of evil. For a Christian, there is only one attitude toward the future. It is hope of salvation.**"* [See endnote, page 330.]

"**Your responsibility is to accept Divine peace, to live it, and to spread it, not through words, but through your life.**"* [See endnote, page 330.]

August, 1984

"The only attitude of the Christian toward the future is hope
of salvation. Those who think only of wars, evils, punishment
do not do well.

"If you think of evil, punishment, wars, you are on the road to
meeting them. Your responsibility is to accept Divine peace,
live it, and spread it."* [See endnote, page 330.]

September 10, 1984

"Dear children, you must understand that one has to pray.
Prayer is no joke, prayer is a conversation with God. In every
prayer you must listen to the voice of God. Without prayer
one cannot live. Prayer is life."

October 5, 1984

"I love you. Love me, love one another."

November 17, 1984

"Pray. Do not ask yourself about the reason why I constantly
invite you to prayer. Intensify your personal prayer so that it
will become a channel for the others."

December 21, 1984

"Dear children! I would like each of you to be like a flower
which is going to open at Christmas for Jesus, a flower which
does not cease to bloom after Christmas. Be the good
shepherds of Jesus."

December 29, 1984

The anniversary of Jelena's first apparition:

"Today is the feast of the Mother of goodness, of mercy, and of love."

Our Lady blessed the group for the first time and they were strongly changed because of it.

"Up until now I have given it to no one."

The group was motivated to receive Our Lady's blessing.

"Receive it, do not neglect it as before. I can give you my blessing, but I cannot give it to you if you do not want it."

To Jelena:

"I wish that a great love, a great peace would flourish in you. Thus, pray."

February 20, 1985

"I give you advice; I would like you to try to conquer some fault each day. If your fault is to get angry at everything, try each day to get angry less. If your fault is not to be able to study, try to study. If your fault is not to be able to obey, or if you cannot stand those who do not please you, try on a given day to speak with them. If your fault is not to be able to stand an arrogant person, you should try to approach that person. If you desire that person to be humble, be humble yourselves. Show that humility is worth more than pride.

Thus, each day, try to go beyond, and to reject every vice from your heart. Find out which are the vices that you most need to reject. During this Lent, you should try and truly desire to spend it in love. Strive as much as possible."

February 25, 1985

"Know that I love you. Know that you are mine. I do not wish
to do anything more for anyone, that I do not wish to do for
you. Come all of you to me. Remain with me and I will be
your Mother always. Come, because I wish to have all of you."

Lent, 1985

"Fast on bread and water during the first week of the Passion
and on Holy Wednesday, Holy Thursday, and Good Friday."

March 25, 1985

Jelena asks why Our Lady is so beautiful:

"I am beautiful because I love. If you want to be beautiful,
love. There is no one in the world who does not desire beauty."

May 3, 1985

"Sometimes prayers said in a loud voice keep Jesus at a
distance, because when men want to conquer with their own
strength there is no place for God. Prayers said out loud
are good when they come from the heart."

May 19, 1985

"Dear children, at this time I ask you particularly to
consecrate yourselves to me and to my Immaculate Heart.
Love, pray, and fast."

June 1, 1985

"Always have the love of God in you, because without this love,
you are not able to convert yourselves completely. Let the
rosary be in your hands in memory of Jesus. Dear children,
strive to go deep into the Mass as you should."

Mid-June, 1985

Our Lady gave Jelena this explanation after she saw a beautiful pear divide itself. Each section glittered and then faded.

"Jelena, man's heart is like this splendid pearl. When he belongs completely to the Lord, he shines even in the darkness. But when he is divided, a little to Satan, a little to sin, a little to everything, he fades and is no longer worth anything."* [See endnote, page 330.]

June 22, 1985

Our Lady inspired Jelena to write down this prayer and to say it in her prayer group:

PETITION TO GOD

**Oh God, our hearts are in deep obscurity,
in spite of our link to Your Heart.
Our hearts are between You and Satan;
do not permit it to be like that!
Every time our hearts are divided
between good and evil,
let them be enlightened by Your light
and let them be unified.**

**Never permit,
for there to be able to exist in us two loves,
that there can never co-exist in us two faiths,
and that there can never co-exist in us:
lying and sincerity,
love and hatred,
honesty and dishonesty,
humility and pride.**

**Help us, on the contrary,
so that our hearts may be elevated toward You**

just like that of a child.
May our hearts be rebuilt and captivated with peace and
continue to always have
the longing for peace.

May Your Holy will and Your love
dwell in us, that at least
sometimes we would really wish to be Your
children and when, Oh Lord,
we will desire to be Your children,
remember our past desires
and help us to receive You again.

We open our hearts to you
so that Your holy love will remain in us.
We open our souls to you,
so that they may be touched by Your holy mercy
which will help us to see clearly all our sins,
and will make us realize
that which makes us impure is sin.

God, we want to be Your children,
humble and devout,
to the point of becoming your cherished and sincere children,
such as only the Father
would be able to desire that we be.
Help us, Jesus, our brother,
to obtain the goodness of the Father in our regard,
and to be good to Him.

Help us, Jesus,
to understand well what God gives us,
although sometimes we fail to perform a good act,
as though it were for us an evil.

This prayer was inspired by Our Lady and She said it was the most
beautiful prayer that could be said for a sick person:

PRAYER FOR A SICK PERSON

O my God,
behold this sick person before You.
He has come to ask You
what he wishes
and what he considers as the most important thing for him.
You, Oh my God,
make these words enter into his heart:
"What is important, is the health of his soul."

Lord, may Your will in everything
take place in his regard, if You want Him to be cured,
let health be given to him;
but if Your will is something else,
let him continue to bear his cross.

I also pray to You for us,
who intercede for him;
purify our hearts,
to make us worthy to convey
Your holy Mercy.

Protect him and relieve his pain.
that Your holy will be done in him,
that Your holy name be revealed through him.
Help him to bear his cross with courage.

Recite the Glory Be three times before this prayer and the preceding one.

June 25, 1985

"A heart which belongs to the Lord is splendid, even if it is flooded with difficulties and trials. But if the heart engaged in difficulties strays away from God, it loses its splendor."

June, 1985

"Dear children, if there is someone and he asks you for something, give it to him. I, too, ask before many hearts, and they do not open up. Pray so that the world may receive my love."

July, 1985

To Jelena's group:

"I cannot speak to you. Your hearts are closed.

"You have not done what I told you; I cannot speak to you. I cannot give you graces as long as you remain closed."* [See endnote, page 330.]

To Jelena's group:

"Each of you has a special gift which is your own and can alone understand it interiorly."* [See endnote, page 330.]

To Jelena's prayer group:

"It seems when you carry my messages, be on your guard that they are not lost. Carry my messages with humility, in such a way that on seeing happiness in you, persons will desire to be like you. Do not carry my messages to simply throw them to others."* [See endnote, page 330.]

July 28, 1985 - August 4, 1985

"During these days, I wish that you consider this idea: After so long and so much time, I have not met Jesus, my friend. After so long and so much time, I have not encountered my Mother, Mary. In these days, I want to encounter them."* [See endnote, page 330.]

August, 1985

"Do not be afraid of Satan. That isn't worth the trouble, because with a humble prayer and an ardent love, one can disarm him."* [See endnote, page 330.]

September, 1985

A prayer given by Our Lady for Jelena's prayer group to say:

"My soul is full of love like the sea. My heart is full of peace like the river. I am not a saint, but I am invited to be one."* [See endnote, page 330.]

October, 1985

On three successive evenings, Jelena was given these messages:

"If you wanted to accept my love, you would never sin."* [See endnote, page 330.]

On the fourth evening in response to Jelena's question about He repeating the same message, Our Lady says:

"But I don't have anything else to say to you."* [See endnote, page 330.]

Crying, Our Lady adds:

"There are many who finish their prayers, even without entering into them."* [See endnote, page 330.]

October, 1985

In response to a question asked by a group of pilgrims from Milan asking when Our Lady would go there:

"When you open your hearts to me."* [See endnote, page 330.]

December 7, 1985

"I have only one wish for tomorrow's feast. I ask of you to find
at least a quarter of an hour for you to come before me and
entrust your problems to me. No one will understand you as
I do."

December 31, 1985

"Next year is the year of peace; not because men have named
it so, but because God has programmed it. You will not have
peace through the presidents but through prayer."

To another of the little seers:

"When you hear the bells at midnight, you will fall on your
knees, bow your head to the ground so that the King of Peace
will come. This year I will offer my peace to the world. But
afterwards, I will ask you where you were when I offered you
my peace."

December, 1985

"If you have not listened to my messages, the day of joy will
become, for me, a day of sadness."* [See endnote, page 330.]

January 21, 1986

During the second day of the prayer group retreat:

"This evening, rest."

January 22, 1986

To the same prayer group:

"I know that you are tired, but I cannot tell you rest. Today,
I tell you, pray, and do not go to bed before having prayed at

least a quarter of an hour for the group. Tomorrow will be a better day."

January 27, 1986

To Jelena's prayer group:

"Every second of prayer is like a drop of dew in the morning which refreshes fully each flower, each blade of grass and the earth. In the same way prayer refreshes man. When man is tired, he gets rest. When he is troubled, he finds peace again. Man renews himself and can, once again, listen to the words of God.

"How the scenery is beautiful when we look at nature in the morning in all it's freshness! But more beautiful, much more, is it when we look at a man who brings to others peace, love, and happiness. Children, if you could know what prayer brings to human beings! Especially personal prayer. Man can thus become a really fresh flower for God. You see how drops of dew stay long on flowers until the first rays of sun come."

Follow up to the January 27, 1986 Message

"Nature, in this way, is renewed and refreshed. For the beauty of nature, a daily renewal and refreshment is necessary. Prayer refreshes man in the same way, to renew him and give him strength. Temptations, which come on him again and again, make him weak and man needs to get from prayer always a new power for love and freshness. This is why [you should] pray and rejoice for the freshness God gives you."

February 22, 1986

Before the blessing at the end of the prayer group meeting:

"Dear children, you will be able to receive Divine love only in proportion to when you understand that, on the cross, God offers you His immense love."

February, 1986

To Jelena and Mirijana:

"Understand that you are nothing, incapable, really nothing. It is the Father who will do everything."* [See endnote, page 330.]

August 11, 1986

"Dear children, open your hearts and let Jesus guide you. For many people it seems to be hard, but it is so easy! You don't have to be afraid because you know that Jesus will never leave you, and you know that he leads you to salvation."

1986

To Jelena's prayer group after fasting and prayer:

"I have listened to your prayer and yet you will not receive what you have wished. You will receive other things because it is not up to you to glorify yourself, but to Me to glorify Myself in you."* [See endnote, page 330.]

"Do not be afraid. Confide yourself to the Father. Pray until you are sure that He guides everything.

"In difficulties, when you carry the cross, sing, be full of joy."* [See endnote, page 330.]

1986

> **"When people ask you to speak about the apparition, say: 'Let us pray together to understand the apparitions of the Gospa.'"*** [See endnote, page 330.]

1986

For Jelena's group:

> **"I beg you, destroy your house made of cardboard which you have built on desires. Thus, I will be able to act for you."*** [See endnote, page 330.]

1986

For Jelena's group:

> **"I wish only that you would be happy, that you would be filled with joy, that you would be filled with peace and announce this joy."**

To the prayer group:

> **"If you would abandon yourselves to me, you will not even feel the passage from this life to the next life. You will begin to live the life of Heaven on earth."*** [See endnote, page 330.]

September, 1986

> **"Today it is not words nor deeds which are important. The important thing is only to pray, to remain in God."*** [See endnote, page 330.]

October, 1986

This message is from Jesus to Jelena:

"I am joyful, but my joy is not complete until you are filled with joy. You are not yet filled with joy because you are not yet at the stage of understanding my immense love."* [See endnote, page 330.]

Undated

Regarding the similarity of the third secret of Fatima and the signs announced at Medjugorje:

"Do not fear anything. You must forget what is behind you in your life. I only want that from now on you be new people. Do not fear anything when I am near you. I love you."

Regarding a discussion with Father Petar Ljubicic and Father Bonifacio:

"It does not suffice to pray. You must change your life, your heart. Love the others, have love for others. Love what you do and always think about Jesus and you will understand what is good and what is bad."

Undated

"I pray for you because I love you. If you want to love, pray for your brothers and sisters. Today many people need lots of prayers. Pray and be a model to others because through you I want to lead people towards the light."

March 1, 1987

"Dear children, sometimes you oppress your hearts with certain things, and this is not necessary. Sometimes you are afraid by this and that. Why do you need that? Who is with Jesus need not fear. Do not worry with anxiety about what will happen tomorrow or in a few years from now. Abandon yourselves to Jesus and only in that way will you be the sheep that follow their shepherd."

April 12, 1987

"If you love from the bottom of your heart, you receive a lot.
If you hate, you lose a lot. Dear children, love makes great
things. The more you have love inside of you, the more you
can love people around you. That is why, pray unceasingly to
Jesus for Him to fill your hearts with love."

May 16, 1987

"O children! Remember: the only way for you to be always
with me and to know the will of the Father is to pray. That is
why I call you today again; don't let my calls be without effect.
Continue to pray in spite of everything and you will
understand the will of the Father and His love.

"Dear children, when God calls men, it is really a great thing.
Think about how it would be sad to let pass those
opportunities that God allows without taking them. So do not
wait for tomorrow or the day after tomorrow. Say 'yes!' to
Jesus now! And may this 'yes!' be forever."

June 16, 1987

"Dear children, my heart is full of grace and love. My heart is
the gift I give you. Be united! Pray together! Love together!"

July 11, 1987

"O children! I want you to live each new day with love and
peace. I want you to be the carriers of peace and love. People
need so much those graces of peace and love, but they have
lost them because they don't pray! Create in your hearts a
permanent prayer, because only thus will you be able to be
prepared vessels. Through prayer your Father will build you
into the vessels He wants. For this abandon yourselves
completely to Him."

July 30, 1987

"Dear children, today I invite you in a special way to pray for the plans of God to be fulfilled: first of all with you, then with this parish which God Himself has chosen. Dear children, to be chosen by God is really something great, but it is also a responsibility for you to pray more, for you, the chosen ones, to encourage others so you can be a light for people in darkness.

"Children, darkness reigns over the whole world. People are attracted by many things and they forget about the more important.

"Light won't reign in the world until people accept Jesus, until they live His words, which is the Word of the Gospel.

"Dear children, this is the reason for my presence among you for such a long time: to lead you on the path of Jesus. I want to save you and, through you, to save the whole world. Many people now live without faith; some don't even want to hear about Jesus, but they still want peace and satisfaction! Children, here is the reason why I need your prayer: prayer is the only way to save the human race."

Date Unknown

The Lord's Prayer and commentary was dictated by Our Lady to Jelena:

"OUR - This is your Father. Why are you afraid of Him? Hold out your hands to Him. [Make a short pause.] OUR FATHER means that He has given Himself to you as Father. He has given you everything. You know that your earthly fathers do everything for you, so much more does your Heavenly Father. OUR FATHER means: I give you everything my child."

"FATHER - Who is this Father? Whose is this Father? Where is this Father?

"WHO ARE IN HEAVEN - [Make a short pause.] This means: your earthly father loves you, but your Heavenly Father loves you even more. Your father can get angry: He does not; He offers you only His love.

"HALLOWED BE THY NAME - In exchange you must respect Him, because He has given you everything and because He is your Father and you must love Him. You must glorify and praise His name. You must say to sinners: He is the Father; yes, He is my Father and I wish to serve Him and to glorify only His name. This is the meaning of 'Hallowed Be Thy Name.'

"THY KINGDOM COME - This is how we thank Jesus and mean to tell Him: Jesus, we know nothing; without Your Kingdom, we are weak if You are not present together with us. Our kingdom passes whilst Yours does not pass away. Re-establish it!

"THY WILL BE DONE - O Lord, make our kingdom collapse. Let Your Kingdom be the only true one, and make us realize that our kingdom is destined to end and that at once, NOW, we allow Thy will to be done.

"ON EARTH AS IT IS IN HEAVEN - Here, Lord, it is said how the angels obey you, how they respect you; let us be like them, too; let our hearts open, too, and may they respect You like the angels do now. And make it possible for everything on earth to be Holy as it is in Heaven.

"GIVE US THIS DAY OUR DAILY BREAD - Give us, Lord, bread and food for our soul; give it to us now, give it to us today, give it to us always; that this bread may become food for our soul, may nourish us, may that bread sanctify You, may that bread become eternal. O Lord, we pray to you for our bread. O Lord, let us receive it. O Lord, help us to understand what we must do. Let us realize that our daily bread cannot be given to us without prayer.

"AND FORGIVE US OUR TRESPASSES - Forgive us Lord our trespasses. Forgive us them because we are not good and we are not faithful.

"AS WE FORGIVE THOSE WHO TRESPASS AGAINST US - Forgive us them so that we, too, may forgive those we were not capable of forgiving until now. O Jesus, forgive us our trespasses, we beseech You. You [meaning us] pray that your sins may be forgiven you in the same measure as you forgive those who trespass against you, without realizing that if your sins were really forgiven as you forgive those of others, it would be a very miserable thing. This is what your heavenly Father is telling you with these words.

"AND LEAD US NOT INTO TEMPTATION - Lord, deliver us from hard trials. Lord, we are weak. Do not let our trials, O Lord, lead us to ruin.

"BUT DELIVER US FROM EVIL - Lord, deliver us from evil. May we succeed in finding something worthwhile in our trials, a step forward in our life.

"AMEN - So be it, Lord, Thy will be done."

NOTES AND FUTURE EXPANSION
OF OUR LADY'S MESSAGES

NOTES AND FUTURE EXPANSION
OF OUR LADY'S MESSAGES

NOTES AND FUTURE EXPANSION
OF OUR LADY'S MESSAGES

NOTES AND FUTURE EXPANSION
OF OUR LADY'S MESSAGES

NOTES AND FUTURE EXPANSION
OF OUR LADY'S MESSAGES

PART III

CONCLUSION:
HOW IMPORTANT IS
MEDJUGORJE
IN THE HISTORY
OF THE WORLD

CONCLUSION

HOW IMPORTANT IS MEDJUGORJE IN THE HISTORY OF THE WORLD?

After reading these messages, you might think that Our Lady's messages are simplistic, that they are not that important, or that they are repetitive. After only one reading, this is understandable; however, Our Lady indicates there are mysteries to be discovered in Her messages.

October 23, 1986

> **"Without your prayer, I cannot help you to understand the messages that my Lord has permitted me to give you."**

Indeed, there is mystery in these messages and the clue to discovering the mysteries is prayer.

Throughout the Sixties and Seventies, the saying, "If it feels good, do it," was popular. It seemed the devil roamed with freedom. Then astoundingly in 1981, Our Lady indicated that A GREAT WAR IS GOING TO TAKE PLACE. Our Lady announces to the earth . . . A DECLARATION OF WAR.

August 2, 1981

> **"A great struggle is about to unfold, a struggle between my Son and Satan. Human souls are at stake."**

As with many of Our Lady's messages, this message, read with prayer and contemplation, is so full of information that after thinking about it, we should realize that we all are underestimating the magnitude of Medjugorje.

In World War II, countries fought for domination. Few complained about being drafted; indeed, many volunteered freely from this country (U.S.A.). They left their jobs, their businesses, their homes to fight. There was no price too high to pay. The volunteerism was so strong it was as if martial law had been declared. Factories changed over to producing arms and the whole country geared up for war without reservations.

Now . . . in 1981, Our Lady states that a full-fledged war is about to start between heaven and hell - not for countries, but for the souls of the earth caught in the middle. A WAR OF THE WORLDS.

As with World War I and II, there is a battle plan with this war also. For three years Our Lady spoke of . . . **"The plan"; "Pray for the plan"; "Pray that Satan does not thwart my plan"; "Pray for the plan My Son and I have"; "Pray that God's plan may be realized."** Then, after three years of speaking of this mysterious plan, She reveals it.

January 25, 1987

> **"Dear children! Behold, also today I want to call you to start living a new life as of today. Dear children, I want you to comprehend that God has chosen each one of you, in order to use you in his great plan for the salvation of mankind. You are not able to comprehend how great your role is in God's design. Therefore, dear children, pray so that in prayer you may be able to comprehend what God's plan is in your regard. I am with you in order that you may be able to bring it about in all its fullness."**

When we refer to a "battle plan" in this context, we do not mean aggressiveness. We define "battle plan" as the sense of mobilization that one needs in his struggle with the devil.

We have to step in combat against Satan, and we have to be ready for sacrifice in this spiritual war. In a message given to the Medjugorje Prayer Group through Jelena, who receives interior locutions, Our Lady says,

July 30, 1987

"Darkness reigns over the world."

We ought to be conscious of this tragic situation of the world today, then we should step in against Satan. How? Our Lady tells us:

August 8, 1985

> **"Dear children, today I call you especially now to advance against Satan by means of prayer. Satan wants to work still more now that you know he is at work. Dear children, put on the armor for battle and with the rosary in your hand defeat him!"**

Our Lady uses words "armor" and "battle" on purpose so we may realize that the activity of Satan is like the invasion of a country by a foreign army. He takes strongholds and destroys. His only purpose is to use us for his own end. His main purpose is destruction. Our Lady gives us five weapons against Satan:

1. Prayer (purification of the spirit)
2. Fasting (purification of the body)
3. Reading of the Bible (purification of the intelligence)
4. Confession (to make God's love grow in us)
5. Holy Communion (to make God's love grow in us)

Our Lady's plan for the salvation of mankind on earth is to defeat Satan using these five weapons. We have to understand that the Medjugorje plan is a plan for the entire planet, that this war is a war of love against destruction, and that Our Lady's goal in this struggle is the reign of love. The Blessed Mother tells us:

November 20, 1986

To Marija:

"You know that I love you and that I am burning out of love for you. Therefore, dear children, you also decide for love so that you will long for and daily experience God's love. Dear children, decide for love so that love prevails in all of you, but not human love, rather God's love."

We have to know that love is our first weapon against Satan because love is the thing he hates and fears the most. Our armor is the fatal weapon of love, and this love encompasses the five weapons against the Ruler of Darkness!

November 25, 1987

Our Lady says that we have to pray,

"So Satan won't attract us in his arrogance and his deceitful vigor."

Satan's weapon is also passivity or indifference "that destroy peace and prayer." That means that the devil is creating a certain inactivity and laziness that attacks the root of conversion; we have to be mobilized always. The victory happens through love and living in holiness.

July 10, 1986

"Today I call you to holiness. You cannot live without holiness. That is why obtain victory against every sin through love. Overcome with love all the difficulties that come to you. Dear children, please, live love inside of you."

In this battle of the "worlds" against Satan, Our Lady puts a weapon in our hands, the only instrument against the powers of darkness, love!

July 31, 1986

> **"Let your only instrument always be love. By love turn everything into good which Satan desires to destroy and possess. Only that way shall you be completely mine and I shall be able to help you."**

God is seeking soldiers to draft - Privates, Captains, Generals. Our Lady tells us our role is "great." One cannot give enough to this plan. We cannot do enough to live the messages. We should be willing to give everything and abandon ourselves completely because in today's WAR OF THE WORLDS, our homes, our money, and our businesses are not important. Only that we love.

All this does not mean to leave your state in life. If you've been given riches, give richly to the plan. If you are talented, use your talents abundantly for this plan. If you are a housewife, give Our Lady the ammunition She needs by praying at your kitchen sink. Everyone has a great role. Remember, Our Lady did more for the Kingdom of God by being a Mother than all the angels, prophets, and mankind together.

Our Lady wants each of us to have a special peace within us. This peace is reflected through our countenance and it will identify whose side we are on. Heaven will win if we write the messages of Our Lady on our hearts and live them.

Once you understand the plans God and Our Lady have for the world today, you cannot overemphasize, over stress, or exaggerate them. We are in the midst of something of such magnitude that there are few other times in human history to which it can be compared.

* ENDNOTE

Not all, but some of these messages are through a third party, usually a parish Franciscan. Some have been mentioned in various talks and may have been reworded from the exact way Our Lady gave them, perhaps for the sake of clarity, for a generalization of the message, or for making a point about a certain subject. The substance of these messages is correct; however, some of these dates may be approximated.

PART II INDEXES

An extensive Index is provided to help you in your research and study. Sometimes the messages of Our Lady can only be remembered through one word. The Word Index was designed with this need in mind. Following the Word Index is a Phrase Index. Also included in this edition is a Chronological Index of Dates for those who remember a message by its date or want to see if a message was given on a particular date. (See Chronological Index for more information.)

At the end of these indexes, we list logical words (which one might think would be in Our Lady's messages) but after searching for them, we found that they were not included in Our Lady's messages. We list them to help you save time in your research.

WORD INDEX

Abandon 91, 134, 135, 146, 167, 185, 229, 232, 235, 238, 259, 270, 273, 276, 283, 284, 291, 316-318

Abandoned 270, 293

Abandons 270

Absorbed 189

Abstain 122

Accept 69, 125, 130, 134, 167, 171, 174, 175, 177, 186, 188, 190, 191, 195, 203, 213, 215, 240, 241, 246, 269, 275, 287, 298, 303, 304, 305, 312, 319

Accepted 137, 163, 195

Accepting 173, 174, 214

Accompany 72, 84, 95, 218, 230, 271

Accomplish 151, 185, 194, 240

Accomplished 110, 133, 137, 195, 272

Account 63, 83, 107, 112, 155, 162, 188

Accumulated 201

Achieve 171, 174, 181, 204

Achieved 296

Acknowledge 135

Acquired 118

PHRASE INDEX

WORDS FROM HEAVEN

CHRONOLOGICAL INDEX (c)

This system of chronologically indexing Our Lady's messages was designed to facilitate the checking of dates to learn what Our Lady was saying during certain events or periods in our lives or in history. For example: If we check dates 7/25/90 - 10/25/90, we can see that Our Lady gave a prophetic message and then continued giving simple messages which had great meaning. During this time, Iraq invaded Kuwait and few realized the global consequences. Looking back on Our Lady's messages, we find them to be simple yet profound. Our Lady did something that has not been done since the beginning of the apparitions. Week after week, Our Lady told Ivan to pray for peace during this time.* This showed that Our Lady knew the danger to the world; however, during this same period, most of us did not understand the extent and depth of the situation as it actually was. You will also find that Our Lady sometimes gave more than one message on the same day. Check the Chronological Index - 12/24/88 (229 and 262). More than one page number after a date generally indicates more than one message given on that day. On 12/24/88, Ivan received a message in Medjugorje while Marija received a message in Alabama, in America. During Marija's apparition, Our Lady gave a Special Blessing.

Studying Our Lady's messages can tell us many things. We pray this Chronological Index will help all of us in our desire to understand Our Lady's messages.

---

* It is reasonable to assume that these messages are mainly about the Middle East crisis; however, one must understand that these are living messages. They have been purposely given by Our Lady with simplicity so that ten years from now this message of peace would speak to us not about the Middle East crisis but about some personal crisis in our lives, our country, the world, etc.

CHRONOLOGICAL INDEX

WORDS NOT FOUND IN OUR LADY'S MESSAGES

The following are words which have been searched for in Our Lady's messages and not found. They are listed to help you save time in your research.

FROM THE TWO AUTHORS

It is felt that the making of this book was the work of the Holy Spirit working through many people. Many messages would not have been preserved had it not been for certain individuals, such as Father Vlassic. We thank those individuals for their many contributions and, in particular, Father Faricy, for his spiritual direction and help regarding Medjugorje, and Father Rene Laurentin, for his diligent investigation of the messages and help which resulted in staying the negative verdict regarding the apparitions and causing the Vatican to step in and continue the investigations.

There are some messages regarding Bishop Zanic that are purposely not published in this book because we feel this book is to be used to help in your conversion. Does this mean other negative messages do not appear in <u>Words From Heaven</u>? <u>No!</u> We print every message we have knowledge of as long as it can be validated from a <u>very</u> reliable source. Bishop Zanic and Our Lady's messages through the visionaries were not printed because the situation is so complicated that to print the messages without a full and complete explanation would be damaging. Not understanding the whole situation would only lead to confusion and possibly hurt your conversion. For this reason, we chose to withhold these messages; however, if you find it necessary to have them for your research, you may order them from Saint James Publishing.

--ORDER FORM--

St. James Publishing
P.O. Box 380244
Birmingham, Alabama 35238-0244

Gentlemen:

   Please send me _____ copy(ies) of WORDS FROM HEAVEN by Two Friends of Medjugorje.

   Enclosed is my payment in the amount of _____. Thank you.

NAME _____

STREET _____

CITY _____

STATE _____ ZIP _____

Payment must be included with order.

PRICE FOR U.S.A. ORDERS

1 Copy $12.00
5-9 Copies $11.00 each
10 Copies or more $10.00 each

Please add $3.00 shipping and handling for each order up to $25.00 going to one address. Add $5.00 for orders up to $100.00, $8.00 for orders up to $300.00, and $12.00 for orders up to $600.00.

PRICES FOR CANADA, MEXICO AND ALL OTHER COUNTRIES

IN CANADA AND MEXICO, the book rates are the same as in the U.S.A. Please add $2 extra to the above shipping and handling charges.

PRICE FOR ALL OTHER COUNTRIES

$23.00 per copy (includes shipping and handling)

For multiple orders or book-store orders, call 800-562-4159 for rates.

PAYMENT FOR ALL ORDERS MUST BE IN U.S. FUNDS

(SOON AVAILABLE IN FOUR LANGUAGES)

--ORDER FORM--

BOOKLETS AVAILABLE

Include Payment When Writing To:
SAINT JAMES PUBLISHING
P.O. Box 380244
Birmingham, AL 35238-0244

The author of these booklets is one of the Two Friends of Medjugorje who wrote the book, <u>Words From Heaven.</u> The information contained in these booklets, in most instances, is first-hand information, written by someone on the inside.

"IN FRONT OF THE CRUCIFIX WITH OUR LADY" - This booklet describes the peace, holiness, and joy available when accepting the crosses which come to us in this life and lists many of Our Lady's messages on this subject. **$1.00**

"A BLESSING TO SAVE THE WORLD!" - This booklet describes the SPECIAL BLESSING which Our Lady has given for our conversion and to be passed on for the conversion of the world. A must for all. **$1.00**

"MEDJUGORJE - THE FULFILLMENT OF ALL MARIAN APPARITIONS?" - This booklet gives new insights and understanding on the connection among all the major Marian Apparitions and how Medjugorje is proving itself to be the fulfillment of all apparitions. **$1.00**

"BISHOP ZANIC - WHAT WENT WRONG?" - This booklet attempts to give some insight into the "why's" of the conflict between the Parish of Medjugorje and the local bishop, Bishop Zanic. **$1.00**

"CHANGING HISTORY" (Western Civilization - Two Choices - Humble Itself or Be Humbled) - This booklet compares the role reversal between the East and the West - the spiritual awakening in the East and the spiritual dying in the West. The West must humble itself or deal with the reckoning of God and be humbled. **$1.00**

"UNDERSTANDING OUR LADY'S MESSAGES" - Insights into the importance, greatness, and magnitude of Our Lady's messages as well as the importance of prayer and child-like receptivity to understand them. **$1.00**

Quantity Discount

10 copies	.70 ea.	100 copies	.45 ea.
25 copies	.60 ea.	500 copies	.40 ea.
50 copies	.50 ea.	1,000 copies	.30 ea.

For U.S.A. Shipping and Handling:

1-5 copies	$1.50	101-300 copies	$8.00
6-25 copies	$3.00	301-600 copies	$12.00
26-100 copies	$5.00	601-1,000 copies	$18.00

For Foreign Rates, Write or Call (205) 672-9596

ALL PAYMENTS MUST BE IN U.S.A. FUNDS

--ORDER FORM--

St. James Publishing
P.O. Box 380244
Birmingham, Alabama 35238-0244

Gentlemen:

Please send me _____ copy(ies) of WORDS FROM HEAVEN by Two Friends of Medjugorje.

Enclosed is my payment in the amount of _____. Thank you.

NAME _____

STREET _____

CITY _____

STATE _____ ZIP _____

Payment must be included with order.

PRICE FOR U.S.A. ORDERS

1 Copy $12.00
5-9 Copies $11.00 each
10 Copies or more $10.00 each

Please add $3.00 shipping and handling for each order up to $25.00 going to one address. Add $5.00 for orders up to $100.00, $8.00 for orders up to $300.00, and $12.00 for orders up to $600.00.

PRICES FOR CANADA, MEXICO AND ALL OTHER COUNTRIES

IN CANADA AND MEXICO, the book rates are the same as in the U.S.A. Please add $2 extra to the above shipping and handling charges.

PRICE FOR ALL OTHER COUNTRIES

$23.00 per copy (includes shipping and handling)

For multiple orders or book-store orders, call 800-562-4159 for rates.

PAYMENT FOR ALL ORDERS MUST BE IN U.S. FUNDS

(SOON AVAILABLE IN FOUR LANGUAGES)

--ORDER FORM--

BOOKLETS AVAILABLE

Include Payment When Writing To:
SAINT JAMES PUBLISHING
P.O. Box 380244
Birmingham, AL 35238-0244

The author of these booklets is one of the Two Friends of Medjugorje who wrote the book, <u>Words From Heaven.</u> The information contained in these booklets, in most instances, is first-hand information, written by someone on the inside.

"IN FRONT OF THE CRUCIFIX WITH OUR LADY" - This booklet describes the peace, holiness, and joy available when accepting the crosses which come to us in this life and lists many of Our Lady's messages on this subject. **$1.00**

"A BLESSING TO SAVE THE WORLD!" - This booklet describes the SPECIAL BLESSING which Our Lady has given for our conversion and to be passed on for the conversion of the world. A must for all. **$1.00**

"MEDJUGORJE - THE FULFILLMENT OF ALL MARIAN APPARITIONS?" - This booklet gives new insights and understanding on the connection among all the major Marian Apparitions and how Medjugorje is proving itself to be the fulfillment of all apparitions. **$1.00**

"BISHOP ZANIC - WHAT WENT WRONG?" - This booklet attempts to give some insight into the "why's" of the conflict between the Parish of Medjugorje and the local bishop, Bishop Zanic. **$1.00**

"CHANGING HISTORY" (Western Civilization - Two Choices - Humble Itself or Be Humbled) - This booklet compares the role reversal between the East and the West - the spiritual awakening in the East and the spiritual dying in the West. The West must humble itself or deal with the reckoning of God and be humbled. **$1.00**

"UNDERSTANDING OUR LADY'S MESSAGES" - Insights into the importance, greatness, and magnitude of Our Lady's messages as well as the importance of prayer and child-like receptivity to understand them. **$1.00**

Quantity Discount

10 copies	.70 ea.	100 copies	.45 ea.
25 copies	.60 ea.	500 copies	.40 ea.
50 copies	.50 ea.	1,000 copies	.30 ea.

For U.S.A. Shipping and Handling:

1-5 copies	$1.50	101-300 copies	$8.00
6-25 copies	$3.00	301-600 copies	$12.00
26-100 copies	$5.00	601-1,000 copies	$18.00

For Foreign Rates, Write or Call (205) 672-9596

<u>ALL PAYMENTS MUST BE IN U.S.A. FUNDS</u>